Ship Rock sailing the high desert under a summer sky.

Mike Butterfield's Guide to the

MOUNTAINS OF NEW MEXICO

Including his photographs and tales of mountain exploration

By Peter Greene

NEW MEXICO
MAGAZINE

Photographer: Mike Butterfield

Editor: Suzan Hall

Executive Editor: Bette Brodsky

Interior maps, book design and production: Bette Brodsky

Copy Editor: Arnold Vigil

Publisher: Ethel Hess

ISBN: 978-0-937206-88-1

Library of Congress Control Number: 2006924457
New Mexico Magazine
495 Old Santa Fe Trail
Santa Fe, New Mexico 87501

Printed in China

Front and back covers: *Alpenglow on the Sacramento Escarpment, from the Tularosa Valley.*

TABLE OF CONTENTS

PROMINENT MOUNTAIN RANGES & OTHER HIGH POINTS:

Truchas Amphitheater in the Pecos Wilderness, Santa Fe Mountains.

Top: *Ship Rock in the Chuska Mountains.*
Bottom: *Rabbit Ears in the Organ Mountains.*

TABLE OF CONTENTS

Top: *Sitting Bull Falls in the Guadalupe Mountains.*
Bottom: *Alpenglow in the Sawtooth Mountains.*

Top: *Near Black Mountain in the Mogollón Mountains.*
Bottom: *Animas Mountains, Gray Ranch Preserve.*
Bottom photo by Peter Greene

ACKNOWLEDGMENTS

First and foremost, I want to thank Waleed Ashoo and the folks at Lithexcel Printing Service for their generosity and support. Without this beneficial partnership over the years, I would probably not be in the wonderful position of publishing this book.

Thanks to *New Mexico Magazine* and to Design Director Bette Brodsky in particular. I feel fortunate to have Peter Greene on board. His writing has brought the mountains to life. I'm grateful to my hiking partners and good friends, Jon Schreiner, Phil Cromer, and Jessie Phillips, for their support and patience while I pursued fine light. Terry Neeld has seen it all. Thanks for sharing high summits and many miles of wilderness trails with me over the years. Bill Maxey, my brother-in-law, has been a great photography partner, and we have shared some grand adventures.

My parents, Bernie and Anne Butterfield, get credit for instilling in me the belief that I could succeed on whatever path I chose, whether it be photography, music or the jewelry business.

Finally, I want to thank my wife, Susan, for her understanding and support. It gets a bit tough having to manage the house, get the kids to school and dance, and teach, while I go galavanting around the state.

This book is dedicated to my daughters, Michelle Byron and Sara Ann Rose.

Mike Butterfield

I would like to acknowledge Steve Cary and my other friends and former colleagues at New Mexico State Parks for all their help and insightful suggestions and thank Bill Clark for recommending me to *New Mexico Magazine* as a potential author. Researching and writing this book has been a great opportunity to reacquaint myself with, and rekindle my passion for, the mountains I've so relished hiking and exploring for the last thirty years. It has also reminded me of what originally lured me here from the comfortable, flat wilds of New Jersey.

Many thanks to my co-collaborators on this project—designer Bette Brodsky and her elegant eye for layout; the supportive *New Mexico Magazine* staff; Suzan Hall, the patient, meticulous editor; and Mike Butterfield, the book's instigator and exuberant mountaineer/photographer/raconteur/altimeter.

Peter Greene

I was shocked into an awareness of mountains. It was 1969, and I was fifteen. We were headed for Breckenridge, Colorado, that year's summer vacation destination. We had driven across the high desert and through the hot San Luis Valley and entered the mountains. At Hoosier Pass, altitude 11,600 feet, Dad stopped so we could admire the view. I was wearing a tee shirt and Bermuda shorts; I hopped out of the car and pretty much froze. That didn't keep me from being impressed with the scenery, though. All about us were great peaks streaked and plastered with snow, each vying for dominance.

I didn't know names or elevations, but knew I wanted to find out more about this land above the trees. It was my first real hint that there was something more to do than hang around in the city. My family had camped in the mountains, but the activity was separate from the scenery. I never really thought about the surroundings. That all changed on Hoosier Pass.

On that same vacation we took a side trip to Tiger, an old mining town, and my cousin and I decided to climb a likely and accessible summit. We climbed only to the 12,574-foot point on the shoulder of Mount Guyot but felt as if we were on the top of the world.

Later, back in Albuquerque, I told one of my brother's friends about this revelation. He informed me that there was a huge wilderness area outside of Santa Fe, full of mountains that reached above timberline. No way, I said. He showed me the map. There it was, a rather large, blank, roadless area, but with elevation numbers that intrigued me: 12,662 feet, 13,102 feet. I had to see what this was about. I discovered the Pecos Wilderness, full of peaks, lakes, and rivers, and I was hooked. Over the next few years I went as often as I could and climbed all of the high peaks, either with friends or, much to my mom's chagrin, alone.

Years in California, pursuing a music career, didn't dampen my enthusiasm for the high peaks. I climbed Mount Shasta and explored throughout the Sierra Nevada and the Trinity Alps. My sojourns in New Mexico were usually punctuated with trips into the Colorado Wilderness.

When my wife and I moved back to New Mexico in 1992, I was afraid that my beloved Pecos Wilderness peaks would somehow be diminished. I need not have worried. The Pecos was as great as I remembered it, and possibly in better shape than when I had left seventeen years before.

Now, thirty-five years after my first mountain encounter, the high peaks are no less spectacular, and I get the same feelings I had as a youth. My good friends and I make annual pilgrimages, and I have introduced my two daughters to the wilderness. I hope to spend many more years climbing and hiking with my friends.

The whole state of New Mexico has opened up to me. Before California my interest was in the northern Rocky Mountains, with their timberlines and spruce forests. Now the southern part of the state, long ignored, is one my main interests. The population is sparse and the open spaces are great. There are mountains of the first order and desert peaks of great grandeur, beauty, and mystery, fine places to explore and photograph.

The idea for this book came from two simple facts: New Mexico is mountainous, and the only comprehensive book on our mountains, Herbert Ungnade's *Guide to New Mexico Mountains*, was written in 1965. I wanted to bring this state's mountainous areas to light in more than a guidebook, and to showcase the beauty and diversity of the major ranges in photographs and stories. Reading this book and looking at the photographs, I hope you find yourself yearning to see these places. My hope in bringing these places more recognition is that we will continue to find it in our best interest to preserve them, for ourselves and for future generations.

Mike Butterfield

South Truchas (13,102'), left, and Cerro Chimayosos (12,841') dominate this early morning scene in the Pecos Wilderness, Santa Fe Mountains. Taken looking north from high on East Pecos Baldy.

DESPITE ITS REPUTATION FOR WIDE SKIES AND OPEN VISTAS, NEW MEXICO IS ANYTHING BUT FLAT. MORE THAN A THIRD OF THE LAND IN THIS STATE IS MOUNTAINOUS, AND THE MEAN ELEVATION IS A HEADY 5,700 FEET ABOVE SEA LEVEL. JUST ABOUT EVERY VISTA IN THIS STATE INCLUDES A MOUNTAIN RANGE.

New Mexico's multihued, multitextured mountains are more than spectacular scenery. They keep this semi-arid state hydrated and irrigated by collecting nearly all its limited rainfall and snowmelt. They provide habitat for a multitude of plants and animals, both common and rare, and are a rich source of renewable natural resources. They offer splendid opportunities for human recreation and renewal.

New Mexico's mountains are remarkably diverse and geologically complex. Mountain building in this state was a lengthy drama in many acts: Vast ancient seas advanced and retreated, depositing a sediment of marine fossils and rocks. Tectonic plates collided, faults opened, volcanoes erupted and spewed lava far and wide. Lengthy cycles of building, erosion, and rebuilding sculpted the ranges, giving each a distinctive face.

The New Mexico landscape began taking its current form twenty-five or thirty million years ago, when the land rose above sea level to stay, tilted from northwest to southeast, as it is today. Around the same time, southwestern New Mexico exploded with volcanic fury, building the massive

Dátil-Mogollón volcanic plateau and, to the east, pushing Sierra Blanca nearly twelve thousand feet into the sky. This volcanic activity and the formation of the Río Grande Rift gave rise to the mighty Sandía, San Mateo, Magdalena and Organ Mountains. The Río Grande Rift, a 600-mile-long tear in the earth's crust that reaches from southern Colorado into Mexico, is one of only five continental rift valleys in the world. It created a long strip of basins in the center of the state through which the Río Grande began flowing only two million years ago.

New Mexico, known as the Volcano State, contains one of the greatest concentrations of young, well-exposed volcanoes on the continent. Here you can see virtually every type of volcanic landform, well-preserved by the semi-arid climate: composite volcanoes, like Sierra Grande and Mount Taylor; lava flows, like the El Malpais; calderas, like the Valles Caldera; ash flows, like the Parajito Plateau in the Jémez Mountains; cinder cones, like Capulín Mountain; volcanic necks, like Cabezón Peak; and clusters, like the Ratón-Clayton volcanic field.

New Mexico is a land of contrasts. Within its boundaries are arid deserts, lush rivers and streams, expansive grasslands, playas and sand dunes, colorful plateaus, rugged volcanic uplands, forested highlands, and twelve-and thirteen-thousand-foot peaks. The state lies at the crossroads of four physiographic provinces: the Rocky Mountains in the north, the Great Plains to the east, the vast Basin and Range in the center and southwest, and the Colorado Plateau to the northwest. Elevations range from 2,817 feet, south of Carlsbad, to 13,161 feet, on Wheeler Peak. The wide range of elevations, landforms, microclimates, and habitats results in a remarkably broad array of ecosystems and wide variety of plants and animals. It is a fine place for hikers and naturalists to add to their life lists of birds, mammals, butterflies, amphibians, and cacti. There are many rare, threatened, and highly localized species, especially in the far southwest Bootheel. Six of the seven life zones found in North America, all but the tropical zone, can be found in New Mexico.

To explore this state's many and varied mountain ranges, we have divided the state into six regions and devoted a chapter to each. The journey begins in northeastern New Mexico, at the end of the Rocky Mountains. The Rockies drop into northern New Mexico in two prongs, on either side of the Río Grande Rift Valley. The eastern prong, New Mexico's Cimarrón and main Sangre de Cristo ranges, enters the state east of the Río Grande and terminates just south of Santa Fe. Although there are impressively high mountains in southern New Mexico, most experts agree that the true Rockies end here.

The western prong of the Rockies is an extension of Colorado's San Juans known in New Mexico as the Tusas Mountains. The best-know features of the Tusas are the Brazos Cliffs and the Toltec Gorge. Prominences connect the Tusas to another volcanic range, the Jémez, the location of the impressive Valles Caldera. Formed by a massive volcanic collapse, it is a valley so vast it can be discerned from space.

The NORTHEAST quadrant of New Mexico is part of the Great Plains province and generally not of great interest to the seeker of heights. There are areas that beckon, however, particularly in the far northeast. Numerous volcanic hills, cones, and mountains dot the landscape, with elevations ranging to 8,700 feet. Capulín Mountain, the best known and a national monument, has an elevation of 8,182 feet and is a cinder cone of nearly perfect proportions. Its summit offers views of eastern Colorado, West Texas, and Oklahoma, and west to the Vermejo plateau of New Mexico. Sugarite Canyon State Park, near Ratón, with its dramatic, caprocked canyons and high mountain lakes, offers welcome relief from the summer heat.

NORTHWEST New Mexico's geologic centerpiece is the San Juan Basin, a part of the Colorado Plateau. Its perimeter of mountains encloses a structural bathtub in which sedimentary rock has been eroded into mesas, buttes, canyons and badlands. Elevations range from 5,000 feet to 11,301 feet, on the summit of Mount Taylor. Throughout the province, volcanic activity is evident; molten material was pushed up through the sedimentary layers and spread over the landscape. The cone of Mount Taylor is the largest extinct volcano in the region, but Ship Rock, with its exposed neck rising seventeen hundred vertical feet above its surroundings, is perhaps the best known.

The peaks in CENTRAL New Mexico tend to be more isolated and more sky island in character. Fault blocks are the main geographic features of the Sandía, Manzano, Los Piños, Sierra Ladrone, Caballo, Fra Cristóbal, San Andrés, Oscura, and Organ Mountains. For the most part, these north-south trending ranges border the Río Grande Rift.

Although altitude in this state generally decreases from north to south, several peaks in SOUTHEAST New Mexico have relief that equals or surpasses that of their northern counterparts. Sierra Blanca (11,993 feet), a volcanic mountain, boasts the greatest relief in the state, rising a full 7,800 feet from its base in the Chihuahuan Desert of the Tularosa Basin to its treeless summit. It is also distinguished by being the southernmost point in the United States that was altered by glaciation. The nearby Capitán Mountains, which rise to 10,201 feet and are famous as the home of Smokey Bear, are unique in being one of the nation's very few east-west trending ranges.

One of the most significant mountainous areas in New Mexico is in the SOUTHWEST within the vast Dátil-Mogollón Volcanic Plateau. This area contains the Gila and San Francisco Rivers, significant waterways in an otherwise arid region. The Black Range, Mogollón, Magdalena, San Mateo, and San Francisco Mountains are heavily forested and contain large roadless areas of declared or de facto wilderness. This most sparsely populated region of New Mexico contains the Gila Wilderness, the first declared wilderness in the country and one of the landmark wilderness ecosystems in the nation. The Gila is on a par with the Greater Yellowstone, North Continental Divide, Central Idaho, Everglades, and North Cascades wilderness complexes.

The sparsely populated, far-southwestern region known as the BOOTHEEL contains some of the most remote, isolated, and biologically diverse areas in the entire state. It is part of the Basin and Range province, and its mountain ranges generally follow a north-south trend. The lowland valleys, or playas, that separate them contain some of the state's best examples of Great Plains grass communities. Several of these sky island ranges are directly connected to Mexico's Sierra Madre Occidental, providing important ecological, cultural and political links with our neighbor to the south.

The inhabitants of this area have been drawn to high places since prehistoric times. The earliest evidence of human occupation in the New Mexico mountains dates to the Clovis period, approximately twelve thousand years ago. Fossils of prehistoric bison, camel, mammoth, and mastodon have been found, intermixed with prehistoric spear points, in Paleoindian sites. Considered sacred by Native Americans, the mountains provided essential shelter, food, refuge, and the raw materials of everyday life. Some prehistoric groups even camped and hunted at elevations of more than ten thousand feet and bagged a high peak or two, as weathered mountaintop shrines attest. Those prehistoric people were New Mexico's first mountaineers.

Sixteenth-century Spanish expeditions led by Coronado, Oñate, and Espejo traversed the New Mexico mountains in efforts to colonize, build missions, and discover gold. Though they did not find much gold, the Spanish did a fair amount of prospecting in the Sandía, Manzano, Jémez, Ladrones, and Ortiz Mountains during their three hundred years of rule. The most successful Spanish mine was the Santa Rita, which was established in 1804 and shipped twenty thousand mule loads of copper down to Chihuahua.

After New Mexico became a US territory, Army geological surveys confirmed that the mountains contained some valuable ores, but it was not until after the Civil War that the big gold and silver strikes were realized. The coming of the railroad in 1878 made mining ventures far more profitable and spurred several booms. During the mining booms, surveying parties under the command of Lieutenant George Wheeler climbed and named many of the state's mountains, including Wheeler Peak. They found that nearly every range in the state contained some useful minerals.

It was not only mineral wealth that attracted adventurers to the mountains in the mid-nineteenth century. The demand for beaver pelts prompted trappers to seek their fortunes along the streams in the Sangre de Cristo Mountains.

Looking north toward Little Costilla Peak across the Valle Vidal, the valley of life. These magnificent parklands, teeming with wildlife, are among New Mexico's crown jewels.

Mountain men like St. Vrain, Antoine Robidoux, and Kit Carson burnished their reputations for bravery here.

In the late nineteenth century the demand for lumber, for house construction and for the railroads, led to substantial timber harvesting. The timber ventures were especially aggressive in the northwestern Zuni Mountains, the Sacramentos, and the Tusas. Fortunately, some of the nation's leading conservationists had the foresight to urge that the mountains' limited natural resources be protected. Because of wise use strategies and the establishment of national forests and federal wilderness areas, most of the unique ecological niches in these mountains remain for us to enjoy.

The intent of this book is to familiarize you with New Mexico's many and varied mountain ranges, with the hope that you will explore them, love them, and care for them. There is much more to these mountains than meets the eye. Take a drive, take a hike, take a photograph of a range you've never seen before. Go back to a place you have been many times, and take a fresh look. You may be surprised at what you discover.

THIS BOOK IS FOR PEOPLE WHO LIKE TO EXPLORE—WHETHER ON THE TRAIL, ON THE HIGHWAY, OR FROM THE COMFORT OF A FAVORITE ARMCHAIR.

It is full of information about the mountains that can be found in every part of this geographically diverse, scenically amazing state. It is designed to give you not only the basic facts about every range, but also its unique flavor.

This is a book to enjoy at home and take with you when you travel. Of course if you are planning a serious outdoor adventure, this is not the only book you will need. You will want to supplement it with a detailed guide to the range or region you plan to visit. *Mike Butterfield's Guide to the Mountains of New Mexico* will help you decide where you want to go exploring, help you get there, and tell you what to look for when you arrive. Most of all, it is put together with the hope that you will fall in love with New Mexico's mountains, just as the authors have. That's why we have included several sources of information:

Peter Greene's text takes your around the state, region by region, starting in the northeast. After an overview of the region, each major range is profiled. These profiles contain intriguing information about how the range was formed, its scenic and wilderness character, and recreational opportunities, as well as fascinating bits of history and lore.

Mike Butterfield's photos provide a sense of place that words could never convey. His essays bring the mountains alive as he invites you to share his adventures backpacking, shooting photos, and bagging 12K peaks.

The bulleted list for each range gives you fast access to information about the roads, the highest and steepest peaks, the hiking trails and wilderness areas, the vegetation and wildlife, and much more. The peak and wilderness lists in the back of the book will tell you where you can find climbing challenges or enjoy the quiet of unspoiled nature.

Numerous maps encourage you to get out on the road and see all these ranges for yourself. The large fold-out map was designed especially for this book by Benchmark Maps, and it shows all the mountain ranges in photographic relief, with elevations. It includes most roads, major towns, Indian pueblos, state parks, and national and state monuments. Country roads, small towns, county lines, and the boundaries of national parks and Indian reservations have been omitted for the sake of readability. If you need more complete road and place information, we recommend the state highway map or Benchmark's wonderfully detailed *New Mexico Road and Recreation Atlas*. On the back of the fold-out map are New Mexico's Scenic Byways and historic trails in relationship to the other major roads and the mountain ranges.

The simple, schematic maps within the book provide at-a-glance information about the ranges, nearby towns, and highways. You will notice that the state has been divided into six regions and each region is color-coded, beginning in the tabel of contents and continuing through the maps and headings for each section. This will enable you to quickly locate the places described in words and photographs.

We hope you enjoy the tour.

ERA	PERIOD	AGE IN MILLIONS OF YEARS	EPOCH
CENOZOIC AGE OF MAMMALS	QUATERNARY	.01	RECENT
			PLEISTOCENE
		2	PLIOCENE
		5	
	TERTIARY	24	MIOCENE
			OLIGOCENE
		37	EOCENE
		58	
		66	PALEOCENE
MESOZOIC AGE OF REPTILES	CRETACEOUS	144	
	JURASSIC	208	
	TRIASSIC	245	
PALEOZOIC AGE OF FISHES	PERMIAN	286	
	PENNSYLVANIAN	330	
	MISISSIPPIAN	360	
	DEVONIAN	408	
	SILURIAN	438	
	ORDOVICIAN	505	
	CAMBRIAN	570	
PRE-CAMBRIAN			

New Mexico is, by and large, a dry state. With scant moisture and high elevations, the sun sears the land. It is subject to the cycle of drought which is persistent throughout the west. Although we are too far inland to feel the full effects of Alaskan Gulf or Pacific weather systems, El Niño in the mid-Pacific usually brings us precipitation and La Niña brings a dry winter and a weak monsoon.

While short-term weather patterns vary (there may be good snow years even during drought cycles), the annual cycle is generally predictable. December, January and February are usually the coldest months, with the greatest snow accumulation. In the northern mountains and the high southern ranges, moderate-to-deep snow packs nourish the land throughout the year.

In early spring temperatures start to climb throughout the state. The snow pack is at its deepest in the high mountains. Temperatures in the desert ranges and valley bottoms are comfortable. This can be a great time to enjoy the outdoors.

Late March through late May is usually windy, as high pressure asserts itself and fronts skirt the northern border of the state. These can be trying times for outdoor ventures. Warming weather and the desiccating winds begin to melt the snow pack.

By late May or early June, the southern mountains have shed their winter snows. The desert can be uncomfortably hot, but the high mountains are cool and comfortable. Trails open up, and springs and seasonal streams are usually running due to the snow melt. This can be a great time to visit the Mogollón Mountains or the Black Range.

Around July 3, moisture buildup and higher humidity at the state's southern borders signal the start of the summer monsoons. They typically reach the Albuquerque area around July 7 and the northern border a few days later. Mornings are usually clear, but by mid-afternoon great cumulonimbus clouds have formed over the mountains and begin drifting over the lower landscape, raking the land with rain as they meander about. The nourishing monsoons supply almost half of New Mexico's annual precipitation, but the amount can vary greatly across the state.

This is the season to be watchful when on high mountains and ridges. It is advisable to get an early start, so as to return before the storms. Getting caught on a high ridge during a severe thunderstorm is an experience best left to the imagination. If you are caught in a storm, it is very prudent to retreat to a lower elevation. Stay away from isolated trees and shallow depressions. If lightning is close, crouch low with only the balls of your feet touching the ground. Lightning is a serious threat; New Mexico ranks second only to Florida in number of strikes, and first in deaths from lightning.

The view from the summit of Tschicoma Mountain (11,561') as summer monsoons rake the land east of the Jémez Mountains.

The monsoon pattern continues, in some form or other, throughout the summer, until the first fronts push the high pressure to the east. Temperatures finally moderate from mid-August into September. These can be calm months, with some of the best weather for hiking and backpacking. The days are usually warm, while the nights become increasingly brisk. With the smell of green chile in the air and a bit of frost to greet the morning sun, fall is probably the best outdoor time of the year.

From mid-October and into November, when the snows begin in the northern mountains, is a fine time to again enjoy the southern ranges. The snow pack usually begins to accumulate in earnest by December. Until spring arrives again, the snow-mantled high mountains are the domain of the winter enthusiast.

Mike Butterfield

Exactly what is a mountain? Everyone would agree about Mount Everest or the Matterhorn; they are tall and pointed, a child's idea of a perfect mountain. But what about more obscure peaks, in ranges that are more rolling and gentle, like the Gallinas Mountains, the Cedar Mountains, or even the Sacramento escarpment?

According to *Encyclopedia Britannica*, a mountain is a large land mass that rises to a point and has an elevation differential that is two thousand feet above its surroundings. This broad definition does not provide any way to measure the overall steepness, or "power," of a given range or peak, because it does not specify the number of miles required to reach the required elevation. Fred Becky, in his *Cascade Alpine Guide* books, uses three miles from base to summit as the benchmark to determine a peak's power. I used both *Britannica's* definition and Becky's standard to measure each mountain range featured in this book, to not only determine elevations but also identify the peak or point with the greatest relief within each range. I used the *National Geographic* topographic software to take the measurements.

This is how I determined, for instance, that the lowest altitude in the Gallinas Mountains is 6,500 feet, reached over a distance of eight miles. With an overall elevation differential of 2,137 feet, the Gallinas qualify as "mountains," but just barely. The greatest relief is 1,906 feet, from the summit of Gallinas Peak. If you are a climber looking for a challenge, the Gallinas don't have a lot of power. The Cedar Mountains didn't even qualify for this book. They rise to over six thousand feet, higher in elevation than many of the ranges we have included, but they measure only 1,415 feet from summit to base before they disappear into the surrounding playa.

But consider the Sacramento Escarpment. It is approximately 6.21 miles from the summit of Alamo Peak, one of the highest points in the Sacramentos, to the valley floor. The overall differential is 4,902 feet. However, measured at three miles Alamo Peak has a relief of just 3,500 feet. Mule Peak, at 8,114 feet, with a relief of just over 3,600 feet at three miles, has the greatest power in the range.

This system helped us decide which ranges to feature in this book, but we made some exceptions (the Tres Hermanas Mountains, for example) and omitted some ranges due to space constraints (The Robledos). If your favorite obscure mountains are not in the book, that is probably the reason.

You'll find three measurements listed for each featured range: the overall elevation, the highest peaks, and the peak with the greatest relief. If you are a hiker or climber, these numbers can tell you at a glance which ranges might be enticing and where you can find the greatest challenges. In any event, enjoy our mountain bounty, and good climbing!

Mike Butterfield

Flanked by West Truchas (13,070) on its left and by unamed 12,885' to its right, North Truchas Peak, at 13,024',is one of the state's highest. Located deep within the Pecos Wilderness of the southern Sangre de Cristo Mountains, it is a true wilderness peak. This view is from the summit of Cerro Chimayosos.

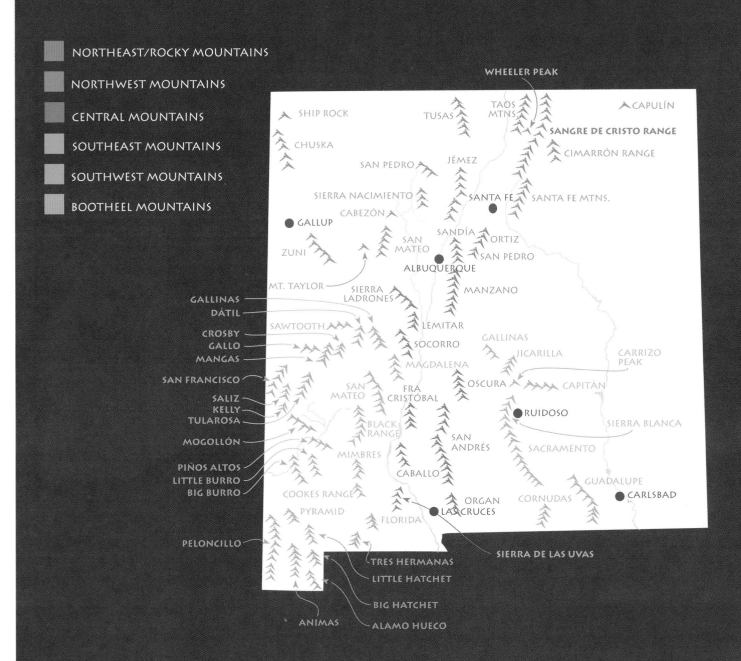

MOUNTAIN RANGES

- NORTHEAST/ROCKY MOUNTAINS
- NORTHWEST MOUNTAINS
- CENTRAL MOUNTAINS
- SOUTHEAST MOUNTAINS
- SOUTHWEST MOUNTAINS
- BOOTHEEL MOUNTAINS

WHEELER PEAK

SHIP ROCK
TUSAS
TAOS MTNS.
CAPULÍN
SANGRE DE CRISTO RANGE
CHUSKA
JÉMEZ
CIMARRÓN RANGE
SAN PEDRO
SIERRA NACIMIENTO
SANTA FE
SANTA FE MTNS.
CABEZÓN
GALLUP
SANDÍA
ORTIZ
SAN MATEO
ZUNI
SAN PEDRO
ALBUQUERQUE
MT. TAYLOR
SIERRA LADRONES
MANZANO
GALLINAS
DÁTIL
SAWTOOTH
LEMITAR
GALLINAS
CROSBY
GALLO
SOCORRO
JICARILLA
CARRIZO PEAK
MANGAS
MAGDALENA
SAN FRANCISCO
OSCURA
CAPITÁN
SAN MATEO
FRA CRISTÓBAL
SALIZ
KELLY
RUIDOSO
TULAROSA
SIERRA BLANCA
BLACK RANGE
MOGOLLÓN
SAN ANDRÉS
SACRAMENTO
MIMBRES
PIÑOS ALTOS
CABALLO
LITTLE BURRO
GUADALUPE
BIG BURRO
COOKES RANGE
ORGAN
CORNUDAS
CARLSBAD
PYRAMID
LAS CRUCES
PELONCILLO
FLORIDA
SIERRA DE LAS UVAS
TRES HERMANAS
LITTLE HATCHET
BIG HATCHET
ANIMAS
ALAMO HUECO

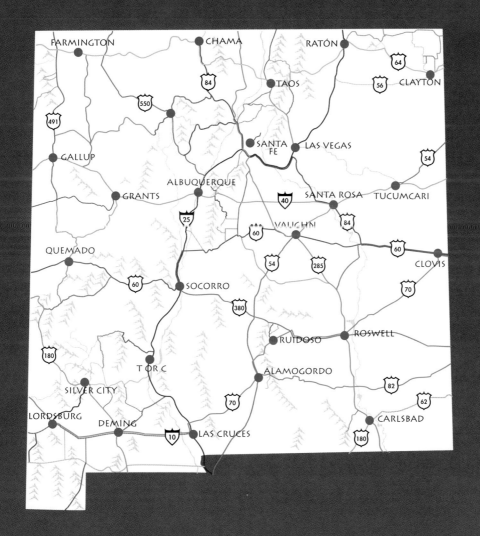

The Jémez Mountains under a deep mantle of winter white, as seen from Pajarito Mountain.

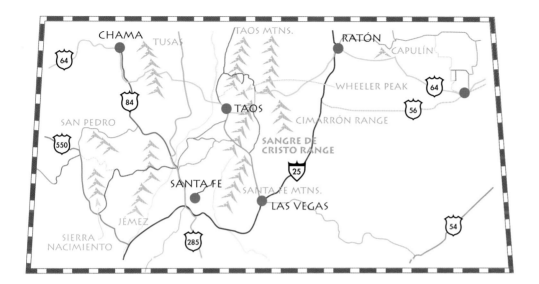

The Sangre de Cristo Mountains, which dominate north-central New Mexico, are the southern terminus of the 3,000-mile-long Rocky Mountain chain. The Rockies, which stretch from northwestern Alaska through the Santa Fe Range east of Santa Fe, took shape during a period of intense plate tectonic activity between forty and seventy million years ago. Most of the high-mountain country in New Mexico lies along the north-south demarcation formed by the Río Grande Rift, a trough which is the result of fractures in the earth's crust some twenty-five to thirty million years ago.

Many small earthquakes along the faults that resulted from those fractures indicate that the rift is still actively evolving. Stay tuned. In the meantime, get out and explore this scenically diverse, geographically lively area.

NORTHEASTERN NEW MEXICO IS A LAND OF GREAT CONTRASTS, AND OF GEOLOGIC DRAMA THAT IS STILL BEING PLAYED OUT TODAY.

This is where the western margin of the Great Plains meets the craggy, twelve- to thirteen-thousand-foot peaks of the Rocky Mountains, and where the Río Grande Rift effectively splits the Rockies then runs south all the way to Chihuahua, Mexico. This is where you can see an array of natural wonders that includes a field of more than one hundred extinct volcanoes, the 650-foot-deep Río Grande Gorge, the vast Pecos Wilderness, the Valle Vidal Natural Area, and the Valles Caldera.

THE RATÓN-CLAYTON VOLCANIC FIELD, LOCATED BETWEEN THE TOWNS OF CLAYTON AND RATÓN, IS ONE OF THE BEST EXAMPLES OF A LARGE VOLCANIC FIELD IN THE WORLD.

It is distinctive for its great size, young age, and continental interior setting. While the Ratón-Clayton volcanic field is not a mountain range or even a series of mountains, it deserves mention here because of its fascinating geologic history and because its numerous volcanic cinder cones create mountainlike relief. It is the easternmost Cenozoic Era (Age of Mammals) volcanic field in the United States and covers nearly seventy-five thousand square miles of northeastern New Mexico and adjoining Colorado and Oklahoma.

Volcanic fields are typically clusters of small volcanoes, up to two miles across, which consist mainly of cinders, splatters, and dark lava flows. The volcanoes were not all formed at the same time; several thousand years may have passed between the eruptions. The earliest volcanic activity on this plateau occurred about 8.2 million years ago, and the Ratón-Clayton Volcanic Field contains more than one hundred basaltic cinder cones created in the past one million years.

Capulín Mountain is one of the youngest volcanoes on the Ratón-Clayton volcanic field. It erupted about sixty-two thousand years ago and has the classic, symmetrical cinder-cone shape. A complicated mosaic of lava flows and cinder/splatter eruptions during and after the initial cinder cone eruption built the volcano we see today. It is distinguished from other volcanoes of this type by its size: nearly a mile across at its base, with a relief of nearly one thousand feet and a summit crater that is more than three hundred feet deep. You don't need to be a hiker to view the Capulín crater. This is one of the few New Mexico volcanoes with a paved road to the summit and a parking lot on the crater rim.

Capulín Volcano attracts a lot more moisture than the surrounding plains and is a relative oasis of vegetation, with pine and juniper trees, wildflowers, shrubs, and moss-covered rocks. Capulín is Spanish for chokecherry, which is found in some abundance on the volcano and the surrounding volcanic terrain.

Sierra Grande, an extinct shield volcano, is slightly higher than Capulín and is the highest peak east of the Rocky Mountain Front Range. It is open to the public for climbing and rewards climbers with great views in all directions.

Some of the best preserved segments of the Santa Fe Trail are on the the Ratón-Clayton volcanic field. Famous volcanic landmarks on the trail are Round Mound, Wagon Mound, and Rabbit Ears Mountain.

Gorgeous, verdant Sugarite Canyon State Park, once the site of a thriving coal-mining camp, is on the western edge of the Ratón-Clayton volcanic field. An extended cliff of basaltic rock columns, often referred to as caprock, is the park's most prominent geological feature. About twelve million years ago, broad sheets of molten lava erupted from a nearby volcano, forming layers of basalt rock ten to a hundred feet thick. Beneath the basalt are layers of sandstone, shale, and coal that contain leaf fossils, tracks of *Tyrannosaurus rex*, and the iridium-rich sediment layer that records the comet or meteor impact that ended the dinosaur era. The park is situated on the Ratón Basin, an upland structural basin that extends from Cimarrón, New Mexico, northeast to Huerfano Park, Colorado.

The mesa complex east of Ratón achieved its lofty position in the landscape not by normal mountain-building mechanics but by landscape inversion.

Though it is not the highest volcano in the Ratón-Clayton Volcanic field, Capulín Mountain (8,182'), with it's nearly perfect proportions, is the best known. It is possible to see four states from its summit. Capulín is protected as a national monument.

The basalts capping the mesas were once molten lava that flowed to low spots in the landscape, where they solidified in valley bottoms. Aggressive erosion in the seam between the Rockies and the Great Plains turned former shale hills into today's Canadian River valley and left the erosion-resistant basalts as today's high spots.

Baldy Mountain (12,441') in the Cimarrón Range catches morning light while the Shuree Ponds in the Valle Vidal remain in shadow.

THE SANGRE DE CRISTO MOUNTAINS, THE HIGHEST AND MOST PROMINENT RANGE IN NEW MEXICO, STRETCH NORTH NEARLY TWO HUNDRED MILES FROM THE FOOTHILLS NEAR SANTA FE AND LAS VEGAS TO SALIDA, COLORADO.

They lie just to the east of the Río Grande Rift in the southern Rocky Mountains and form part of the western boundary of the Great Plains. They are characterized by high summits such as Wheeler Peak (13,161 feet) and the three Truchas Peaks (all more than 13,000 feet), deep gorges that cut through sandstone and limestone rock, and lots of faults in the rock that form steep slopes and cliffs. The northern part of the range was shaped by volcanic activity, and the higher elevations have been further modified by glaciers.

The ancient basement rocks of northern New Mexico— granites and metamorphic rocks—formed more than one billion years ago. These rocks were later uplifted to form the cores of the Sangre de Cristos. Erosional resistance of these crystalline rocks supports the high peaks. About 250 million years ago, the ancestral Rocky Mountains were pushed up in about the same place as the modern Rocky Mountain Front Range, which includes the Sangre de Cristos. Erosion eventually wore the ancestral Rocky Mountains down to low hills and plains. The last mountain-building events extended from 170 million to 40 million years ago and formed the fundamental structures of the modern Sangre de Cristos.

By 30 million years ago, local crustal dynamics changed from compression to extension, and the Río Grande Rift began to open up west of the Sangre de Cristo Mountains. Widespread magma intrusions and volcanic eruptions took place in New Mexico. The Río Grande Rift zone has been relatively stable since then, except for a dramatic crustal uplift of the entire southern Rocky Mountains and Colorado Plateau regions. The Sangre de Cristo mountains were pushed up from the earth's surface essentially as one big chunk of rock. Vertical movement exceeded one mile and brought these mountains to their prominent height. Rivers responded to this uplift by entrenching deep canyons such as the Río Grande Gorge of the Taos Plateau.

The Sangre de Cristos are extensive enough that they are typically divided into subranges: the Taos Mountains, the Santa Fe Mountains, which include the Pecos Wilderness, and the Cimarrón Range. The mountains near Las Vegas, New Mexico, are generally considered an extension of the Santa Fe Mountains. The Culebra Range, in extreme northern New Mexico, is primarily a Colorado range and has not been described in this book.

Pueblo Peak (12,305') from the summit of Lake Fork Peak in the Wheeler Peak Wilderness. Seen from the other side, Pueblo Peak is "the view" and the symbol of the city of Taos. Locally known as Taos Mountain, it is located on Taos Pueblo land and is closed to the public.

The name Sangre de Cristo, which means blood of Christ in Spanish, refers to the reddish light cast on the mountains at sunset. There is no consensus as to who first coined the evocative name, but theories abound. It may have been a priest named Juan, mortally wounded in the Pueblo Revolt in 1680, or the Spanish explorer Antonio Valverde, in 1719, or the Penitentes, a religious order devoted to the passion and death of Christ. Other scholars have attributed the name variously to a creek, a pass, and a Spanish military outpost, all in the northern part of the range. Early Spanish documents referred to these mountains as La Sierra Nevada, the snowy range; La Sierra Madre, the mother mountains; or simply La Sierra. Early English-speaking trappers called them the Snowies.

The Sangre de Cristo Mountains, with their great abundance of deer, elk, bear, and turkey, were important hunting grounds for Native Americans. The first Spanish excursion into these mountains was the De Vargas expedition in 1696. The demand for beaver pelts, to make stovepipe hats, prompted the first thorough exploration of these mountains by trappers in the early 1800s. Between 1821 and 1823, some one hundred trappers collected furs in the Pecos and Río Grande valleys. By 1826, the beaver was nearly extinct in the area.

When gold was found in the Moreno Valley, near the Cimarrón Range, in 1866, thousands of prospectors swarmed into the valley and adjacent mountains. A decade or so later, gold was discovered at Twining and Red River prompting extensive prospecting in the valleys. Other ores besides gold were mined in the Sangres, including molybdenum, zinc, and lead. Some of those mining ventures are still in operation today.

The first recorded ascents of the major peaks are credited to surveyors under the command of US Army Lieutenant George Wheeler. Survey parties climbed the Truchas Peaks, Wheeler Peak, Lake Peak, and Santa Fe Baldy between 1873 and 1875. An important event for the Sangre de Cristos, near the turn of the twentieth century, was the establishment of national forests. This new federal policy protected the forests and watersheds and established regulations for grazing, timber cutting, mining, and recreational activities.

31

The high peaks of the Wheeler massif as seen from Old Mike Peak. This view takes in the rugged headwall above Williams Lake and includes, from left, Fairchild Mountain (12,819'), Vallecito Mountain on the distant horizon (12,643'), and Lake Fork Peak (12,881').

LOCATION: Between Costilla and Tres Ritos

ACCESS: US 64; NM 38, 150, 522, 578

ELEVATION: 7,000' - 13,161'

GREATEST RELIEF: Pueblo Peak, 4,785'

MAJOR PEAKS: Wheeler Peak (13,161'), Mount Walter (13,133'), Old Mike Peak (13,113'), Lake Fork Peak (12,881'), Gold Hill (12,711'), Latir Peak (12,708'), Lobo Peak (12,115')

MAJOR ATTRACTIONS: Taos, Taos Pueblo, Río Grande Gorge

HIKING: Wheeler massif: Bull of the Woods, Williams Lake, Lost Lake. Latir massif: Heart Lake, Latir Peak, Baldy Mountain. Hundreds of miles of maintained trails crisscross the region, allowing access to most areas with high peaks.

WINTER ACTIVITIES: Taos and Red River downhill ski areas and Enchanted Forest cross-country area allow access to much of the high country in and around Wheeler Peak and the Columbine-Hondo area. Backcountry areas are prone to avalanche danger and should be approached with great care. Bull-of-the-Woods yurt above Taos Ski Valley is an excellent overnight destination for timberline tours to Gold Hill or Wheeler Peak. Shady Brook Cross-country Ski Area, off highway 64, offers eight miles of moderate to steep skiing. Amole Canyon Cross-country Ski Area is located at the junction of NM 518 and Forest Road 703.

VEGETATION: Engelmann spruce, sub-alpine fir, alpine tundra, aspen, bristlecone pine

WILDLIFE: Elk, deer, black bear, mountain lion, beaver, turkey

WATER: Cabresto Creek, Costilla Creek, Río Hondo, Río Pueblo de Taos. Red River is the principal waterway in the Latir-Gold Hill area. The valley of the Río Pueblo separates the Taos Mountains from the Santa Fe Mountains. There are dozens of other mountain streams and mountain tarns in timberline cirques and forested valleys.

SEASON: Lower elevations are open by mid-May, with higher elevations free of snow by mid-June. First snow is usually by mid-October.

WILDERNESS: Latir Wilderness (20,506 acres, with 146,000 additional acres roadless), Wheeler Peak Wilderness (19,150 acres with 57,000 additional acres roadless), Columbine-Hondo Wilderness Study Area (30,500 acres).

ADMINISTRATION: Carson National Forest, Questa Ranger District, and the private Río Costilla Livestock Association, Latir area

THE TAOS MOUNTAINS CONTAIN SOME OF THE HIGHEST PEAKS AND OLDEST EXPOSED ROCKS IN THE ENTIRE STATE.

Wheeler Peak, at 13,161 feet, is the highest peak, but lesser known Mount Walter and Old Mike Peak are nearly as tall. As for the rocks, some of the igneous types visible on the highest peaks were formed 1.8 billion years ago. Some of these ancient rocks can be clearly seen on the top of Wheeler Peak, at Taos Ski Valley, in the towering cliffs near Pilar, and at Red River Pass. The Taos area is exceptionally dynamic and exciting geologically. Evidence of catastrophic seismic and igneous events visible from the Taos Mountains include young fault scarps where the mountains join the plains and an abundance of volcanoes and basalt flows on the plateau. The ancient Taos area landscape featured mighty Precambrian mountain belts, shallow tropical seas, vast sand deserts, and extensive white sand beaches.

The Taos Mountains, a subrange of the Sangre de Cristos, lie between the Culebra range to the north and the Santa Fe Mountains to the south. They are characterized by steep slopes, alpine lakes, expanses of tundra, and dense coniferous forests. The two designated wilderness areas in the Taos Range—Latir Peak Wilderness and Wheeler Peak Wilderness—have spectacular wild and scenic values and are popular with hikers and climbers. Wheeler Peak was named after US Army Lieutenant George M. Wheeler, who directed surveys west of the one hundredth meridian between 1871 and 1878 and mapped much of New Mexico.

The Taos Mountains, with their abundance of wildlife and minerals, attracted mountain men and prospectors in the nineteenth century. With the Louisiana Purchase in 1803, the mountain man period began in earnest. The popularity of tall beaver-skin hats in the eastern United States brought trappers to the Taos Mountains' plentiful high-country streams. The trappers were bold, eccentric men from all walks of life and cultural backgrounds. Kit Carson was the most famous mountain man in the area.

Mountain men often lived closely with Native Americans and learned their methods of hunting, trapping, and living off the land. It was a precarious way of living, however. Risks included grizzly bear maulings, rattlesnake bites, drowning, climbing accidents, and illnesses such as dysentery and smallpox.

Minerals in the Taos Mountains have attracted attention since prehistoric times. Native Americans used the natural clay and mica for making pottery and many lithic materials for crafting tools, knives, weapons, and personal adornment. The gold placers, particularly at Arroyo Hondo, were said to have been worked by the Spanish long before the Pueblo Revolt of 1680.

Many pioneer trailblazers, including Kit Carson and Lucien Maxwell, were involved in mining and prospecting in the Taos Mountains. The greatest influx of prospectors came after the Civil War, when copper and gold placer were discovered in places like Arroyo Hondo, Red River, Gold Hill, Twining, Black Copper, and Amizette. Despite all the prospecting, exploration, and mining development, the Taos Mountains yielded relatively little high-grade gold or copper. It was not until the 1920s that the most lucrative minerals were discovered and developed: mica, molybdenum, beryl, and optical calcite.

Wheeler Peak (13,161'), the highest point in New Mexico, reaches into a cerulean sky.

Above: *The Río Grande near Pilar is popular with kayakers and rafters during spring and summer runoff. The peaks bordering this section of the river, though not high in elevation, are extremely rugged.*

Opposite: *Morning light on Latir Mesa, as seen from Heart Lake in the Latir Wilderness. With numerous peaks over 12,000', the Latir Range is one of the highest in the state.*

Columbine (Aquilegia caerulea) *blooms on a rocky aerie while nourishing summer monsoon rains replenish the distant upper Pecos Watershed in the Pecos Wilderness.*

LOCATION: Between Santa Fe and Las Vegas, north to Tres Ritos

ACCESS: I-25; NM 50, 475, 63, 76, 65, 518; numerous Forest Service roads

ELEVATION: 6,600'-13,102'

GREATEST RELIEF: Santa Fe Baldy, 4,100'

MAJOR PEAKS: South Truchas (13,102'), West Truchas (13,066'), North Truchas (13,024), Cerro Chimayosos (12,841'), Jicarita (12,835'), Santa Fe Baldy (12,622'), East Pecos Baldy (12,529'), Lake Peak (12,409'), Hermit's Peak (10,212')

MAJOR ATTRACTIONS: Pecos Wilderness, Pecos National Historical Park, Santa Fe, Hyde Memorial State Park, Santa Fe Ski Area, Morphy Lake State Park

HIKING: Over 400 miles of trail crisscross the region, making loop trips and extended stays possible. Highlights include Winsor-Puerto Nambé Trail, Hamilton Mesa, East Pecos Baldy, Truchas Peak, and Hermit's Peak.

WINTER ACTIVITIES: Downhill and cross-country skiing and snowshoeing. Easiest access from the south is through Cowles. The road is generally plowed, although the roads leading to the major trailheads will not be plowed. The easiest, shortest approaches to some of the high peaks are from the Santa Fe Ski Area. The Santa Fe Ski Road is plowed through winter.

VEGETATION: Engelmann spruce, subalpine fir, alpine tundra, aspen, bristlecone pine

WILDLIFE: Elk, deer, black bear, bighorn sheep, mountain lion, marmot, pika, ptarmigan, turkey

WATER: Pecos River, Mora River, Río Santa Barbara, Río Trampas, Río Medio, Río Valdez; numerous creeks, streams, and timberline lakes; and Pecos Falls, a well-watered region that receives over 35 inches of precipitation annually.

SEASON: Lower elevations are open by early May, although north-facing slopes could still have significant snow cover. The higher elevations may not be snow free until mid-June. First snows arrive in late September, or by mid-October.

WILDERNESS: Pecos Wilderness (222,673 acres, with 177,000 additional acres of roadless area)

ADMINISTRATION: Santa Fe National Forest (Las Vegas, Pecos, and Española Districts), Carson National Forest (Camino Real District)

THE SANTA FE MOUNTAINS ARE THE SOUTHERNMOST SUBRANGE OF THE SANGRE DE CRISTO MOUNTAINS AND THEREFORE OF THE ENTIRE ROCKY MOUNTAIN CHAIN.

Like the Taos Mountains, the Santa Fe Mountains contain some of the loftiest peaks in the state and some of the most spectacular mountain wilderness scenery. The Santa Fe Mountains include the mountains by Santa Fe and Las Vegas, the Truchas Peaks, and the Santa Barbara high country. The mountains span the Santa Fe and Carson National Forests and are an integral part of the 222,000-acre Pecos Wilderness.

The Pecos Wilderness is second only to the Gila in size and is considered one of the state's crown jewels. The Pecos is well known for its rugged peaks above timberline, steep-walled canyons, long and broad mesa tops, heavily forested slopes, and lush meadows. Elevations range from 8,400 feet to over 13,000 feet. South Truchas Peak, at 13,102 feet, dominates the northern part of the wilderness. Many of the Pecos Wilderness streams have their headwaters there. To the west, steep-walled canyons drain toward the Río Grande, while to the east lies the relatively gentle Upper Pecos River Valley, an area of flat mesas and grassy meadows.

The wilderness encompasses foothills, montane, subalpine, and alpine life zones. Forests of piñon and juniper transition to ponderosa pine, limber pine, bristlecone pine, aspen, fir, and spruce as the elevation increases. This diversity of vegetation supports a wide variety of mountain wildlife, including Rocky Mountain bighorn sheep and some highly specialized species adapted for the higher elevations of the Pecos, such as the ptarmigan, a ground-dwelling bird; the pika, a small member of the rabbit family; and the yellow-bellied whistling marmot. More than fifteen lakes and eight major streams provide a diversity of riparian habitat and support several different species of trout, including the Río Grande cutthroat, New Mexico's state fish.

For centuries, the Santa Fe Mountains and the Pecos high country have been major resources for Native Americans. Various Pueblo groups, the nomadic Utes and Apache, and the Indians of the Great Plains took full advantage of the area's abundance to hunt, fish, cut wood, and gather medicinal and edible plants. To the south, the Towa Indians inhabited the pueblo the Spaniards called Pecos, likely a Keresan word meaning "place where there is water." The name was also applied to the nearby river and eventually to the wilderness area. When the Spaniards arrived in 1540, they established villages around the wilderness and used the mountain resources much as the Native Americans had. Until the mid-1800s, the nearby settlements and Indian groups had relatively little impact on the high-mountain wilderness. However, following the American annexation of New Mexico in 1846, an influx of English-speaking settlers had a much more profound impact on the resources with grazing, mining, and hunting. By the early twentieth century, all the elk, big-horn sheep, and grizzly bear either had been wiped out or had disappeared.

Fortunately, some farsighted conservationists acted in time to stave off further resource degradation. In 1892, President Benjamin Harrison proclaimed the Upper Pecos watershed a timberland reserve for watershed protection, and the area was closed to logging, grazing, mining, and the public in general. The Pecos Primitive Area of 133,640 acres was established in 1933, declared a Forest Service wilderness in 1955, and made part of the Wilderness Preservation System on September 3, 1964, when President Lyndon Johnson signed the Wilderness Act into law. The Upper Pecos River, from its headwaters to Terrero, was added to the Wild and Scenic Rivers system in 1990. One of the visionaries in preservation was Elliot Barker, who, during his 101 years of life, did more for preserving the wilderness and wildlife of the Pecos than anyone else.

Indian paintbrush near the summit of Santa Fe Baldy frames this view of Lake Peak (12,409') and Penitente Peak (12,249') across the valley of the Puerto Nambé in the Pecos Wilderness.

Opposite *At the end of another beautiful day: Santa Fe Baldy (12,622') and the Truchas Peaks on the far horizon, from high on the shoulder of Lake Peak.*

Right: *South Truchas Peak (13,102'), in sublime alpenglow, reflected in lower Truchas Lake, deep in the Pecos Wilderness.*

The Cimarrón River, on its way to a rendezvous with the Canadian River, flows through the narrow confines of Cimarrón Canyon, which is bordered by the Palisades.

LOCATION: Between Cimarrón and Eagle Nest, running north to Colorado

ACCESS: US 64; NM 21, 434

ELEVATION: 8,200'-12,584'

GREATEST RELIEF: Baldy and Touch-Me-Not, 3,640'

MAJOR PEAKS: Little Costilla Peak (12,584'), Baldy Mountain (12,441'), Touch-Me-Not Mountain (12,045'), Clear Creek Mountain (Mount Phillips) (11,730'), Agua Fria Peak (11,086')

MAJOR ATTRACTIONS: Cimarrón Canyon State Park, Eagle Nest Lake State Park, Angel Fire Ski Resort, Philmont Boy Scout Ranch, Valle Vidal Recreation Area

HIKING: Palisades for rock climbing

WINTER ACTIVITIES: Angel Fire Ski Resort, cross-country skiing. The Val Verde ski area, although located in the Taos Mountains, is accessed from the Moreno Valley above Ildewild on NM 127 near Eagle Nest. Ice fishing is quite popular on Eagle Nest Lake. The entire Moreno Valley is accessible by highway, though private ownership limits access.

VEGETATION: Engelmann spruce, sub-alpine fir, alpine tundra, aspen, bristlecone pine

WILDLIFE: Elk, deer, black bear, mountain lion, antelope, beaver, turkey

WATER: Cimarrón River, Ute Creek, Rayado Creek, Ponil Creek, Willow Creek, Eagle Nest Lake

SEASON: Lower elevations are open by mid-May, with higher elevations free of snow by mid-June. First snow is usually by mid-October. The entire area becomes snow-bound by early November.

WILDERNESS: Colin Neblett Wildlife Area, Philmont Scout Ranch, Clear Creek Mountain (14,290 acres not inventoried). No declared wilderness.

ADMINISTRATION: New Mexico State Parks Division, New Mexico Department of Game and Fish, private ownership (limited access) and Beaubien-Miranda (Maxwell) Land Grant

---

CIMARRÓN, SPANISH FOR WILD AND UNTAMED, REFERRED TO THE WILD BIGHORN SHEEP AND, LATER, HORSES AND CATTLE THAT ROAMED THESE MOUNTAINS.

This narrow, north-south range forms the eastern boundary of the Moreno Valley and continues north almost to the Colorado state line. The mountains were uplifted slowly throughout the Middle and Late Tertiary Period, about twenty million years ago, and feature many beautiful sandstone cliffs. Cimarrón Canyon was formed when volcanic activity blocked south-flowing drainage of the Moreno Valley. The rising waters eventually found a new outlet near Eagle Nest, carving the deep chasm that we can drive through today.

Among the most spectacular geologic features of this range are the sheer walls of crenulated granite called the Palisades, where the turbulent flow of water has broken the rock into massive angular boulders. Expert rock climbers enjoy scaling the challenging, 400-foot-high cliffs. Permits are available from Cimarrón State Park, where the Palisades are located. Cimarrón Canyon is part of the 33,116-acre Colin Neblett Wildlife Area in the central Cimarrón Range, the largest such area in the state.

The 100,000-acre Valle Vidal Unit of the Carson National Forest, a lush mountain basin in the heart of the Cimarrón Mountains, is deservedly renowned for its wildlife habitat and prize elk herd. It contains the headwaters of numerous streams and tributaries of the Río Grande and Canadian Rivers and peaks including Little Costilla (12,584 feet) and Vermejo (11,610 feet) and is widely popular for its recreational opportunities. Donated to the public by the Pennzoil

Company in 1982, it is currently being managed by the Carson National Forest as a multiple use area for sportsmen, recreation enthusiasts, cattle ranchers, and wildlife viewers. The Valle Vidal was historically referred to as the valley of life.

The Cimarrón Mountains and surrounding lands were originally part of the Sangre de Cristo Land Grant given to fur traders Beaubien and Miranda in 1841. When they were killed in the Taos Revolt of 1847, Lucien Maxwell acquired the grant and established a trading post. According to an 1850 survey, the grant was 1.7 million acres. The Ute, Jicarilla Apache, and other Native Americans who considered the grant land their traditional use area continued to hunt in the mountains and traded with Maxwell, occasionally bartering gold nuggets. They also traded at nearby Fort Union. In 1866, a Native American brought copper ore to the fort from the top of Baldy Mountain, a site later developed as the famous Mystic Lode.

When gold was discovered in the sands of Willow Creek, hordes of men swarmed into the Moreno Valley in search of fortune. By 1868, Elizabethtown was established. Numerous mining districts followed. One of the richest mines, the Aztec in Ute Creek Valley, produced more than $3 million dollars worth of ore.

End of Season

October is the end of the season in the Rockies. One late October, two friends and I backpacked to the Truchas Lakes in the Pecos Wilderness hoping to climb the Truchas Peaks one last time before winter closed off the wilderness. The first day, we hiked to Pecos Baldy Lake—a long, uphill workout, but worth it because the of the way the scenery improves, from transitional forest to alpine environment. East Pecos Baldy, with its face of white quartzite, looked spectacular as usual, steep and inviting. Pecos Baldy Lake filled its glacial basin and was the color of a Kashmir sapphire, a deep milky blue and full of mystery. It is an altogether beautiful setting that always lets us know we have arrived in the high country. The weather was fine, if a bit cold at 11,400 feet.

Frost greeted us the next morning as we broke camp for the hike up to and across the great treeless expanse of Trailriders Wall. By first light, the frost had given way to a fine fall day. As the day progressed, lowering clouds began to form. It was pleasant when the sun was out, but when the clouds enveloped it the temperature dropped and the landscape turned ominous. Lower Truchas Lake was somber when we arrived in the early afternoon, the water a dull grey, but we were cheered by the prospect of climbing South Truchas the next day.

By morning, the sky was very threatening. Where we were camped at the lake, at 11,870 feet, the weather held, but the peaks were hidden by heavy cloud cover down almost to the lake level.

There would be no peak bagging that day. We decided to give it a day and hope this was just a passing front, not the first major storm of the season. To our relief, the skies were clearing the next morning, but the storm had dropped several inches of snow almost to the lake level and the temperature had fallen. Clouds scudded across the sky, shredded by the summits of South and Middle Truchas Peaks. We could see that the wind was blowing hard up there, and any summit attempt would be futile.

We decided a prudent retreat was in order. We broke camp and took the lower route back to Pecos Baldy Lake, because it was still free of snow. Trailriders Wall, close on our right side and high above us, was coated in white. The clouds returned with a vengeance. For the rest of the hike, the sunshine was interrupted by dull-gray, lowering clouds, snow squalls and wind. The snow started to accumulate. We never saw Pecos Baldy again on that trip; the front consumed the mountain. We had set out on a day full of promise for a late-season climb and returned, just four days later, through a landscape turned white by several inches of snow. Indian summer had been transformed into Old Man Winter. We made the six-mile hike back to Cowles in snow, then steady rain, and arrived wet but happy, looking forward to the spring day when the high country would once again be open. The peaks would await our return. October is indeed the end of the season.

Mike Butterfield

The Jémez Mountains look their lush-green best after the summer monsoons. This is the view southwest from the summit of Tschicoma Mountain.

LOCATION: West of the Española Valley from Cerro Pedernal, west of Abiquiú to Borrego Mesa, near Jémez Pueblo

ACCESS: NM 4, 290; Forest Roads 289, 142, 268, 136, 269, 10, 137

ELEVATION: 5,300'-11,561'

GREATEST RELIEF: Tschichoma, 3,295'

MAJOR PEAKS: Tsichoma (Santa Clara Peak) (11,561'), Redondo Peak (11,254'), Polvadera Peak (11,232'), Cerro Toledo (10,925')

MAJOR ATTRACTIONS: Bandelier National Monument, Puyé Cliffs, Valles Caldera, Fenton Lake State Park

HIKING: Many hikes in Bandelier National Monument, Sanchez Canyon and Picacho Trail in Dome Wilderness, Vacas Trail, Continental Divide Trail, Vega Redonda Trail in San Pedro Parks Wilderness

WINTER ACTIVITIES: NM 4 provides access to southside trail heads. Pajarito Mountain Ski Area and Camp May, near Los Alamos, have excellent downhill skiing, cross-country, and snowshoeing. Cross-country skiing and snowshoeing by reservation in the Valles Caldera National Preserve. Hall Baxter memorial ski trail at Fenton Lake State Park. Ice fishing on Fenton Lake.

VEGETATION: Piñon-juniper woodland, ponderosa pine, mixed conifer, scrub oak, aspen

WILDLIFE: Elk, deer, black bear, mountain lion, antelope, beaver, turkey

WATER: The Jeméz River is the principal watershed for the region. Río Frijoles and Río Guadalupe are significant secondary waterways. The Río Grande defines the southern boundary. There are numerous streams throughout the region, as well as Fenton Lake and Santa Clara Pueblo ponds

SEASON: Lower elevations, year round. Higher elevations are usually snow free from late May through mid-November.

WILDERNESS: Valles Caldera (89,000 acres) is managed as a trust with limited access. Chama River Canyon Wilderness (50,300 acres), Dome Wilderness (5,200 acres), Bandelier National Monument (32,727 acres). Approximately 83,000 acres of uninventoried roadless parcels in the Polvadera, Lobato, Bearhead Peak, and Mud Springs Area.

ADMINISTRATION: Santa Fe National Forest, National Park Service (Bandelier National Monument), Valles Caldera Trust

IMMENSE VOLCANIC ACTIVITY CREATED THE JÉMEZ MOUNTAINS AND THE PAJARITO PLATEAU. THE MOUNTAINS WERE CREATED ABOUT THIRTEEN MILLION YEARS AGO.

Then, when the Río Grande Rift opened, lava that spewed from vents in the earth created the basalt layers visible at the eastern edge of Bandelier National Monument, and ash flows formed the welded tuff of Frijoles Canyon. Finally, during two periods of mammoth explosions 1.4 and 1.1 million years ago, a magma chamber beneath the layers erupted, ejecting enormous quantities of ash around the margins of the volcano that formed a plateau a thousand feet thick, extending over four hundred square miles. Scientists at Los Alamos, which sits on that plateau, have detected a persisting magma chamber that is the continuing source of hot springs and geothermal energy exploration.

The fourteen-mile-wide Valles Caldera, the largest and most active of New Mexico's dozens of calderas, was formed when the core of the spent volcano finally collapsed. In all of North America, only the Yellowstone Caldera is larger and more active. The tallest summits of the Jémez are on the eastern rim and the southwest edge of the caldera. Volcanic formations extend for miles in all directions, and there are hot mineral springs at Sulphur Springs and in the Valle San Antonio in the caldera. After seeing those springs in 1598, the Spanish explorer Oñate called the Jémez the "mountains of brimstone."

The Jémez Mountains and environs have been inhabited since ancient times. The steep cliffs provided shelter and a high vantage point to spot potential enemies, and the soft volcanic rocks provided building materials for structures. Game was abundant in the forests, and crops could be cultivated in the fertile soil of the canyons. A fluted point found on the plateau suggests Paleoindian occupation as early as ten thousand years ago. Archaeological findings indicate a large population during the Pueblo Period, from 1250 to 1500 AD. Numerous ruins, caves, and petroglyphs are still visible. Some of the best-preserved are in Bandelier National Monument and at the Puyé Cliffs. Ancient trails are everywhere, and Native Americans still use the shrines on the mesas and summits. Jémez Pueblo is still very active.

Since prehistoric times, the Jémez Mountains have been known as a source of obsidian and chalcedony. Gold was found at Bland, south of Valle Grande, in 1889, and subsequently the area yielded over $2 million worth of gold

The Valles Calderas National Preserve, one of the world's largest caldera valleys, was formed by the collapse of a series of volcanoes. Under private ownership for years, this prime wildlife area was finally purchased by the federal government and is now open to the general public on a limited basis. This peaceful sunrise view belies its violent past.

and silver. The Wheeler survey parties climbed the Jémez Mountains in 1873-75.

In 2000, an 89,000-acre property that had been known as the Baca Ranch since the 1850s came into the public domain as the Valles Caldera National Preserve. Situated inside a collapsed crater, it is studded with eruptive domes and contains Redondo Peak (11,254 feet). The preserve is being developed to explore a new way of managing public lands and is open to the public on a limited basis for hiking, fishing, hunting, wildlife observation, and winter sports. The Jémez Mountains also contain the Dome Wilderness Area southwest of Bandelier National Monument, the Chama River Canyon Wilderness north of Abiquiú, and the San Pedro Parks Wilderness near Cuba.

LOCATION: Northwest of San Ysidro

ACCESS: US 550; NM 126, 96, 485

ELEVATION: 7,300'-10,605'

GREATEST RELIEF: At unnamed 10,260' point, 2,900'

MAJOR PEAKS: San Pedro Peak (10,605'), Nacimiento Peak (9,801), San Miguel Peak (9,473), Pajarito Peak (9,042')

MAJOR ATTRACTIONS: Fenton Lake State Park, Jémez Falls, Jémez State Monument, San Pedro Parks Wilderness

HIKING: Vacas Trail, Continental Divide Trail, and Vega Redonda Trail

WINTER ACTIVITIES: Good cross-country skiing and snowshoeing. Gentle gradients in San Pedro Parks allow for extended tours into the wilderness. NM 126 is plowed to at least the San Gregorio Reservoir turnoff. 2.5 miles of skiing to the wilderness boundary.

VEGETATION: Spruce, fir, ponderosa pine, scrub oak, aspen

WILDLIFE: Elk, deer, black bear, coyote, fox, bobcat, beaver, blue grouse

WATER: Río Puerco, Rito de las Vacas, Río Gallina. Well watered, with numerous streams and creeks throughout the region. San Gregorio Reservoir, on the south side of San Pedro Parks Wilderness.

SEASON: Best in summer and fall.

WILDERNESS: San Pedro Parks Wilderness (41,132 acres)

ADMINISTRATION: Santa Fe National Forest (Cuba Ranger District)

THE SAN PEDRO MOUNTAINS AND SIERRA NACIMIENTO ARE CONTIGUOUS, RELATIVELY HIGH ELEVATION, LOW-RELIEF MOUNTAINS LOCATED TO THE NORTHWEST OF SAN YSIDRO.

The San Pedro Parks Wilderness Area sits atop the Sierra Nacimiento, an igneous uplift that rises abruptly from the mesas and plains to the west. While these mountains abut the Jémez Mountains, they are geologically different. The volcanic rocks of the nearby Jémez are generally soft and permeable, but the Sierra Nacimiento are composed of hard, Precambrian granite with an overlay of sedimentary strata in which marine fossils can be found.

Open, gentle parkland and forested ridges await visitors to the surprisingly beautiful and serene San Pedro Parks Wilderness in the San Pedro Mountains. These mountains are geologically different from the larger Jémez Range to which they are linked.

Because the Sierra Nacimiento is where the first high upland storms hit as they come across the Colorado Plateau from the west, the San Pedro Parks Wilderness receives an abundance of rainfall—about thirty-five inches a year. This explains the lush forests and meadows, streams, and drainages. The San Pedro Mountains, north of the Sierra Nacimiento, have rounded, gentle contours and resemble hills more than mountains. Perhaps this is why in the Navajo language these mountains are referred to as "big buttocks place."

The San Pedro Parks Wilderness Area was designated a wilderness in 1931, and it is administered by the Santa Fe National Forest. While it is not particularly well-known, it does have outstanding wilderness characteristics, despite some livestock grazing, and its inviting high upland meadows are attractive and easy to hike. The average elevation of the San Pedro Parks Wilderness is ten thousand feet, and its verdant meadows and marshes are surrounded by mountains of varying steepness.

LOCATION: Between Tierra Amarilla and Tres Piedras

ACCESS: US 64, 285, 84; NM 17; Forest Roads 133, 87

ELEVATION: 7,500'-11,403'

GREATEST RELIEF: Brazos Cliffs, 3,008'

MAJOR PEAKS: Grouse Mesa (11,403'), Brazos Peak (11,288'), San Antonio Peak (10,935'), Canjilón Mountain (10,913')

MAJOR ATTRACTIONS: Brazos Cliffs, Brazos Box, El Vado and Heron Lake State Parks; Sargent Fish and Wildlife Area; Cumbres & Toltec Scenic Railroad

HIKING: Tony Márquez Trail, Toltec Gorge

WINTER ACTIVITIES: US 64 cuts across the mountains east-to-west and provides access to miles of cross-country skiing and snowshoeing. Popular with snowmobilers.

Cumbres Pass (in Colorado) is popular with snowmobilers and skiers. Chama Valley backcountry trails, home to New Mexico Chile Classic.

VEGETATION: Spruce, fir, ponderosa pine, piñon-juniper woodland, aspen, high grassland

WILDLIFE: Elk, deer, black bear, coyote, fox, bobcat, beaver, blue grouse

WATER: Río Chama, Río Brazos, Río de los Piños, Río Vallecitas. Heron and El Vado Lakes, though west of the mountains, are associated with the region. Canjilón, Trout, and Lagunitas Lakes are high-elevation ponds accessible by vehicle. Numerous streams and creeks run throughout the region.

SEASON: Mid-May through mid-November.

WILDERNESS: Cruces Basin Wilderness (18,902 acres), Canjilón non-inventoried roadless area (30,000 acres), Jawbone Mountain non-inventoried roadless area (17,000 acres), Edward Sargent Wildlife Area

ADMINISTRATION: Carson National Forest; Tierra Amarilla Land Grant, access restricted

Opposite: *The Tusas Mountains, mostly characterized by high, rolling, forested plateau, are cut by the deep gash of the Brazos Box. The spectacular Brazos Cliffs greet visitors entering the Chama River Valley.*

THE TUSAS MOUNTAINS IN NORTH-CENTRAL NEW MEXICO ARE A SOUTHERN CONTINUATION OF THE SAN JUAN MOUNTAINS IN COLORADO.

Tusas is Spanish for prairie dogs. This range has also been referred to in the past as the Brazos or Cumbres Mountains. Las Tusas Mountains are characterized by high plateaus of forests and alpine meadows, shaped by glaciers during the Pleistocene Era. These mountains are cored with ancient granite and metamorphosed sedimentary rock. The surface reveals a soft pinkish sandstone, rich in tuff from volcanic ash, which originated from eruptions in the San Juan Mountains to the north and west.

The range is also known for the spectacular Brazos Cliffs and Brazos Box, the Toltec Gorge, and the Cruces Basin Wilderness Area. The precipitous Brazos Cliffs, which form the western edge of the Tusas Mountains, are composed of 1.8 billion-year-old granite and quartzite, some of the oldest and hardest rock in New Mexico. The vertical relief from the summit to the base of the cliffs is more than 2,000 feet, a radical change from the 7,500-foot agricultural lands of the Río Chama Valley. The Brazos Cliffs are very popular with rock climbers. This is also the location of the Brazos Falls, the highest waterfall in New Mexico. The Brazos Box, south of the cliffs on the Río Bravo, is a cliff-walled canyon three times deeper than the Río Grande Gorge. About one million years ago a lava flow cascaded into the Brazos Box, and the dark columnar basalt is visible in the road cut. The Cruces Basin Wilderness, near the Colorado border, is characterized by a patchwork of meadows, aspen groves, and forests, with an abundance of wildlife.

Long before the Spaniards arrived, the Utes, Jicarilla Apaches, Navajo, and Pueblo Indians hunted and foraged in these mountains. In 1832, the Mexican government made a large community land grant to Manuel Martínez and other settlers, which became known as the Tierra Amarilla Land Grant. The threat of Indian attacks slowed Hispanic settlement of the area for many years. In July of 1848, there was a major encounter between the United States Army and a large group of Utes and Jicarilla Apache, during which the famous scout and guide Old Bill Williams was wounded. The army established Fort Lowell in Tierra Amarilla in 1866 to protect the area settlements from the southern Utes. It was garrisoned by a detachment of New Mexico Volunteers but abandoned some three years later.

The lowest of the Canjilón Lakes is at an elevation of nearly 10,000' in the Tusas Mountains. These high-country lakes are locally popular but not well-known outside the region.

Looking east from the summit of Mount Taylor (11,301') into the ancient volcano's caldera, with the Sandía Mountains on the distant skyline.

THE SAN JUAN BASIN, A VAST, SCULPTURED REGION OF SPARSELY VEGETATED PLATEAUS, HIGH MESAS, DEEP CANYONS, GAUNT VOLCANIC NECKS, AND COLORFUL BADLANDS FILLED WITH GEOLOGICAL ODDITIES, DOMINATES NORTHWESTERN NEW MEXICO.

These oddities include the El Malpais lava flow, the Bandera Crater and Ice Caves, La Ventana Arch, the Bisti/De-Na-Zin Wilderness with its eerie mushroom-shaped spires, and those stately sentinels in the desert, Ship Rock and Cabezón.

Physiographically, the entire region lies within the Colorado Plateau, a high-standing block of the earth's crust that covers 140,000 square miles in the Four Corners region of Utah, Colorado, Arizona, and New Mexico. In New Mexico, the

Colorado Plateau has two faces: In some places broad, sage-covered expanses of sedimentary rock erode away into jagged badlands; elsewhere, lava-capped mesas covered in piñon, juniper and ponderosa pine descend precipitously to volcanic plugs, cinder cones, and lava flows. Cabezón Peak, in the Río Puerco Valley between the Sierra Nacimiento and San Mateo Mountains, is one of fifty volcanic plugs that have been exposed by erosion in the Mount Taylor volcanic field.

Mount Taylor in the San Mateo Mountains, at 11,301 feet, is the highest peak in the region. The other ranges in the northwest quadrant, the Zuni Mountains and the Chuska Mountains, do not have the dramatic ragged peaks and plunging streams of the Sangre de Cristos or the Gila, but instead have a gentle, rounded, mysterious beauty created by volcanic activity, lava flows, and red sandstone.

Once you get past the clusters of oil and gas rigs in the San Juan Basin, you'll enjoy this area's multi-hued mountains and bizarre geologic features.

Intense alpenglow on Tse-Bidahi, *the Rock with Wings (7,178'). Also known as* Ship Rock, *this volcanic neck has a two-masted summit that rises 1,700' above its surroundings east of the Chuska Mountains.*

SHIP ROCK, ONE OF THE MOST FAMOUS LANDMARKS IN NEW MEXICO, IS A SHEER, SOLITARY HUNK OF ROCK THAT RISES SOME SEVENTEEN HUNDRED FEET ABOVE THE DESERT FLOOR ON THE NORTHERN EDGE OF THE NAVAJO NATION.

Ship Rock is a remnant of an explosive volcanic eruption that took place about thirty million years ago. It is a volcanic neck, the central feeder pipe of a larger volcanic landform that has eroded away. It is composed of fractured volcanic rock crosscut by many thin veins of lava. Ship Rock may have been one thousand meters below the land surface at the time it was formed, and has since gained its prominence due to the erosion of surrounding rocks.

A striking feature of Ship Rock is the wall-like sheets of lava, called dikes, that radiate away from the central neck. Dikes are formed when a forceful eruption creates fissures in surrounding bedrock. Lava, pushing vertically through the horizontal layers, fills the fissures. Like the neck, the dikes have become exposed as the surrounding rocks eroded.

Anglos first called this volcanic neck The Needle, a reference to the pinnacle at its top. US Geological Survey maps indicate that the name Ship Rock came into use in the 1870s because the formation resembled a nineteenth century clipper ship. The Navajo know Ship Rock as *Tse-Bidahi*, the rock with wings, a representation of the great bird that brought them from the north. It is a sacred place to the Navajo, which is why climbing on it and the other volcanic plugs on the reservation is no longer allowed. The town of Shiprock is the official gateway to the Navajo Nation.

Ship Rock was once considered one of America's toughest mountains. Various attempts to climb its ragged edges were made in the 1930s, but the first successful climb to the 7,178-foot summit was made by four Sierra Club members in 1939. It was subsequently summitted more than one hundred times before climbing was prohibited in 1970.

SHIP ROCK

Todacheene Lake is at almost 9,000' elevation in the heavily forested, well-watered Chuska Mountains.

LOCATION: North of Gallup on the Arizona border

ACCESS: NM 134; Indian Route 13

ELEVATION: 6,000' - 9,783'

GREATEST RELIEF: New Mexico: Beautiful Mountain, 2968'

MAJOR PEAKS: New Mexico: Beautiful Mountain (9,388'), Chuska Peak (8,795'), Ship Rock (7,178')
Arizona: Roof Butte (9,783'), Matthews Peak (9,511')

MAJOR ATTRACTIONS: Chaco Culture National Historical Park, Canyon de Chelley National Monument, Window Rock

HIKING: No designated trails. Any hiking or climbing activities require prior permission from the Navajo Nation.

WINTER ACTIVITIES: Narbona (Washington) Pass area should allow access to cross-country skiing, especially the north road leading to Todacheene Lake.

VEGETATION: Ponderosa pine, aspen, gambel oak, spruce, fir, piñon-juniper woodland

WILDLIFE: Elk, mule deer, black bear, mountain lion, bobcat, coyote

WATER: Numerous lakes, including Toadlena, Todacheene, Berlund north of Narbona (Washington) Pass, Lake Long and Whiskey Lake south of Narbona Pass, and many creeks, including Bull Canyon and Oak Creek, which drain on the west side in New Mexico, and Tsaile Creek in Arizona. The eastern escarpment is much drier.

SEASON: Spring through fall

WILDERNESS: No roadless areas of significant size.

ADMINISTRATION: Navajo Nation

NAVAJO NOVELIST IRVIN MORRIS DESCRIBED THE CHUSKA MOUNTAINS AS AN "ARCHIPELAGO OF WELL-WATERED ISLANDS IN THE HIGH DESERT."

Located northwest of Gallup on the reservation, they comprise the Navajo Nation's wettest and greenest terrain; much of the reservation's surface water is generated in the high ponderosa pine forests.

The Chuska Mountains are an upwarped plateau that towers above the surrounding eroded landscape of the San Juan Basin. The uplift pushed the pinkish Chuska sandstone into the position of the dominant rock unit, now at elevations as high as nine thousand feet. In a few areas, subsequent volcanic eruptions have covered the surrounding sandstones with harder volcanic basalts. On the west base of the mountains are remnants of ancient volcanic activity in the form of necks, lava flows, and layers of volcanic ash. On the east side, the mountains are veneered with landslide deposits of boulders.

It is conjectured that Chuska comes from the Navajo word for white spruce. Escalante used the name and it appears on the map from his famous 1776 expedition. Chuska Peak is especially sacred to the Navajo. They consider it to be, quite literally, the head of this mythic range, just as Narbona Pass is its neck. In 1935, the Navajos demonstrated their reverence for Chuska Peak by blocking the installation of a fire tower on its summit.

The forests of the Chuskas and the nearby Defiance Plateau in Arizona have been important to indigenous peoples of the Colorado Plateau for thousands of years. Archaeological and historical evidence indicates that the Ancestral Pueblo people harvested huge quantities of ponderosa pine from the Chuska's eastern slopes to build massive wood and masonry structures at their ceremonial and trading complex at Chaco Canyon. No one is certain how this large amount of lumber was transported forty or fifty miles across the San Juan Basin to Chaco. Navajos today continue to use the Chuskas for grazing livestock, gathering medicinal herbs and building materials, hunting, and fishing.

There are mysteries in the Chuskas. In recent years, scientists have searched in these and other New Mexico mountains for evidence of Sasquatch, the legendary Bigfoot. There have been reports of sightings, and of Sasquatch taking sheep and goats from local herds, by police officers, game wardens, ranchers, and residents. The researchers have gone so far as to use a combination of human and great ape sex pheromones to draw Sasquatch within observation range. To date, nothing definitive has come of these efforts. If you want to know more, check the BFRO (Bigfoot Research Organization) Website, www.bfro.net.

Between Two Worlds

Not many people are aware of the Chuska Mountains in the Navajo Nation, and I suspect even fewer, outside of the Navajo, have visited them. They are fairly high and wooded, and their most prominent feature is a huge volcanic plug a bit to the east of the main ridge known as *Tse-Bidahi*, the rock with wings. Navajo lore says that *Tse-Bidahi* brought the Diné, the first Navajo people, from the north to their present homeland. To the Anglo this imposing peak is Ship Rock, a two-masted schooner sailing the New Mexican desert. For years it was the premier climbing challenge in the United States.

I set out to capture the mountain on film at that most ephemeral of moments, alpenglow. I worked my way up the south dike emanating from the peak, which culminates in a narrow wall of eroded lava, and found a nice seat for the show, my legs dangling on either side of the wall. To my left was a drop of almost a hundred feet to where the eroded rock met the lava dike. To my right the drop was only thirty or forty feet, but as I was close to three hundred feet above the flat it was a most delicious site. Before me stood Ship Rock in all of its vertical glory, its two main summits towering over the landscape. As I sat there thinking what a fantastic place it was, I noticed a black dot far to the east. I watched as it grew larger and realized it was a man on a horse. He rode straight to the base of Ship Rock, slowed to a walk, and headed for my jeep. Was I was going to be vandalized? No, the chap circled my car, dismounted and started up the slope heading straight towards me. A tribal policeman coming to give me a citation? I extricated myself from my perch and headed down to meet him.

Turned out he was just a young Navajo out for a ride. He didn't speak English, but it was plain that we had something in common: the peak. We finally managed to communicate and, it turned out, he just wanted some water. I gave him what I had. He drank, thanked me, and rode away. I stood there thinking what a great thing had happened. Neither of us spoke the other's language, yet we connected. To the Diné, *Tse-Bidahi* is sacred, special. To the rest of us, it is a marvel to wonder at, try to climb and classify. But it just is. One mountain, two cultures. It's all beautiful.

Mike Butterfield

The Zuni Mountains, just south of I-40 but often ignored by travelers, are surprisingly beautiful and invite exploration.

LOCATION: Between Grants and Gallup

ACCESS: I-40; NM 53, 400; Forest Roads 178, 180, 447, 49

ELEVATION: 6,400' - 9,256'

MAJOR PEAKS: Mount Sedgwick (9,256'), Lookout Mountain (9,112')

GREATEST RELIEF: Mount Sedgwick, 1,934'

MAJOR ATTRACTIONS: El Malpais National Monument, El Morro National Monument, Bluewater Lake State Park, Acoma Pueblo

HIKING: Mount Sedgwick, Cottonwood Canyon, Gallo Peak, Rivera Canyon, Continental Divide Trail

WINTER ACTIVITIES: Some cross-country skiing. Long approaches over unpaved roads may limit access to skiable terrain.

VEGETATION: Ponderosa pine, alligator juniper, gambel oak, spruce, fir, piñon-juniper woodland, aspen

WILDLIFE: Bats (20 different species), jackrabbits, raccoons, weasels, elk, mule deer, black bear, mountain lion, bobcat, fox

WATER: Bluewater Lake, Ramah Lake, McGaffy Lake, Bluewater Creek, Cottonwood Canyon, Río Nutria. There are numerous meltponds and seasonal creeks scattered throughout the region.

SEASON: Lower elevations, year-round. Upper slopes south side are open by mid-April, north slopes by mid- to late May. Snows close access in mid- to late November.

WILDERNESS: No declared wilderness. Oso Ridge roadless (not inventoried), approximately 13,000 acres.

ADMINISTRATION: Cíbola National Forest

THE ZUNI MOUNTAINS CONTAIN SOME OF THE OLDEST EXPOSED ROCK IN NORTHWESTERN NEW MEXICO.

They were carved from a northwest-southeast uplift, are approximately sixty miles long and forty miles wide, and are cored with billion-year-old granite. They are surrounded by and interspersed with younger red sandstone cliffs. Elevations range from 6,400 to 9,000 feet. The gentle upwarp is of the plateau type, primarily of light-colored sandstone, with steep cliffs and deep canyons.

Captain Clarence Dutton, surveying for the US Geological Service in 1879, declared that the Zunis were only "a broad elongate dome almost completely ringed by high inward-facing cliffs. The declivity is gentle and its surface is heavily timbered, so that the eye sees little else than a forest…the platform named Zuni Mountains is not a proper mountain range."

The Continental Divide snakes through the Zuni Mountains, which also harbor isolated volcanic cinder cones and ancient lava flows. The Zuni Mountains are considered the southern boundary of the San Juan Basin, an area known for production of oil, natural gas, uranium, and coal. An interesting footnote is that these mountains seem to attract meteors. At least three struck in the early twentieth century, and some of the fragments were purchased by the Smithsonian Museum.

Native Americans, including the Zuni, Navajo, and Acoma Indians, have used the resources of the Zuni Mountains for centuries and continue to do so. They hunted bear and deer, foraged for wild plants, gathered obsidian for points and tools, and also mined copper and turquoise. The mountains are sacred to the Acoma Indians, who believe the Rainmaker of the West resides here; the average rainfall is twenty-four inches per year.

The Spaniards traveled though these mountains on their way to Zuni Pueblo but made no attempt to exploit the resources or colonize. Pedro Castañeda, a chronicler of the Coronado expedition, conducted the first biological survey of the Zuni Mountains in 1540. He noted there were lots of cranes, geese, blackbirds, and wild turkey.

In the 1890s, the coming of the railroad prompted large-scale logging in the Zuni Mountains, first for railroad crossties, then for cut lumber, doors, moldings, and boxes. American Lumber Company, at its peak around 1910, produced sixty million board feet of timber, employed seven hundred loggers, and shipped one hundred carloads of logs a day. The heavy harvesting took a tremendous toll and hardly a tree or blade of grass was left by the 1940s. Fortunately, Forest Service reforestation, reseeding projects, and sustained yield practices have allowed the mountain forests to make a comeback. The Zuni Mountains, incorporated into Zuni National Forest in 1909, are now a unit of the Cíbola National Forest.

The 1916 Homestead Act brought a wave of settlers to the Zuni Mountain area. Broad green valleys, rich soil, and abundant rainfall make this area well suited for agriculture, especially for cultivating wheat, oats, barley, and rye. The Zunis became known as the breadbasket of western New Mexico. Copper mining was also highly productive from 1916 into the early 1930s. When the defense industry needed fluorspar during World War II, the Navajo Fluorspar Company opened three mines on the east side of the Zuni Mountains. The mines operated from 1940 until 1952.

The south side of the Zuni Mountains, comprised of Zuni sandstone, contains numerous pinnacles and mesas. Perhaps best known is a jutting bluff called El Morro or Inscription Rock, a watering spot where early Spanish and American travelers left their names.

69

LOCATION: Northeast of Grants

ACCESS: I-40; NM 547, 605, 279; Forest Roads 453, 451, 193

ELEVATION: 6,300' - 11,301'

GREATEST RELIEF: Mount Taylor, 3,065'

MAJOR PEAKS: Mount Taylor (11,301'), La Mosca Peak (11,036')

MAJOR ATTRACTIONS: El Malpais National Monument, Bluewater Lake State Park, Acoma Pueblo

HIKING: Mount Taylor/Gooseberry Spring Trail, Water Canyon Trail, Lobo Canyon, Guadalupe Canyon

WINTER ACTIVITIES: Cross-country skiing, snowshoeing. Forest Roads 193 and 547 should allow access to skiable terrain. Site of the Mount Taylor Quadrathlon in February.

VEGETATION: Ponderosa pine, gambel oak, Engelmann spruce, Douglas fir, piñon-juniper woodland, aspen

WILDLIFE: Abert's squirrel, porcupine, gray fox, weasel, skunk, elk, mule deer, black bear

WATER: Goosberry, Cienega, Colorado, Cañocito Springs, Water Canyon (east side), Rinconada Canyon (south side), Lobo Canyon (west side). Check with the Forest Service for the status of all springs.

SEASON: Lower elevations, year-round. Upper slopes are open on the north side by May and on the south side by mid-to late May. Snows close access in mid- to late November.

WILDERNESS: No declared wilderness. Mount Taylor (10,500 non-inventoried acres) is roadless, but the top is subject to off-road vehicle use from the access road to the La Mosca-Mount Taylor saddle.

ADMINISTRATION: Cíbola National Forest

Opposite: *The view from Mount Taylor's summit (11,301'), which is lightly visited despite its impressive stature and regional visibility.*

This upland is called the Mount Taylor volcanic field because it is topped by towering, pyramid-shaped Mount Taylor, which was built from numerous successive lava flows and ash falls starting about four million years ago. For two million years thereafter it erupted repeatedly, unleashing stiff lava domes, releasing lava flows, and spewing out huge hot clouds of volcanic ash. Cinder cones decorate its flanks. Mount Taylor, known as Turquoise Mountain by the Navajo, is the second-largest preserved young volcano in New Mexico, after the Valles Caldera. It is a classic example of a composite volcano, and the way it erupted is frequently compared to the Mount St. Helens eruption in 1980.

Besides Mount Taylor, the San Mateo Mountains consist of a platform of basalt-capped, eight-thousand-foot mesas: Mesa Chivato, La Jara Mesa, San Fidel Mesa, and Horace Mesa. In Spanish times, both the plateau and the mountain were named Cebolleta, which means tender onion. Later the plateau was known as Mesa Chivato, and the mountain was named Mount Taylor in honor of President Zachary Taylor in 1849. Currently, the range that includes Mount Taylor is called the San Mateo Mountains by most authorities, although some still refer to the mountains as the Cebolletas

or simply Mount Taylor. If this isn't confusing enough, there is another San Mateo range in Socorro County.

Navajos have lived on and around Mount Taylor since at least the sixteenth century. The Spanish moved into the area in the 1700s, unsuccessfully attempted to convert the Navajos, established a mission in 1746 and issued land grants to private individuals in the 1760s. The Spanish settlers raised churro sheep and long-legged Mexican cattle, animals hardy enough to handle drought and rough terrain. The Navajos came to resent the settlers' encroachments and began raiding the ranchos and settlements. The raids and settler counterattacks lasted for decades, and both sides resorted to taking slaves.

There was also some logging and mining around Mount Taylor, but it was never as intense or destructive as it was in the Zuni Mountains. Even today, Mount Taylor, with all its prominence on the horizon, is lightly used and seldom crowded compared to the nearby Sandía and Jémez Mountains. The area is well-suited for hiking, mountain biking, cross-country skiing and snowshoeing.

LOCATION: Between Albuquerque's West Mesa and Mount Taylor, near Grants

ACCESS: US 550; County Roads 279 and 39, Cabezón Road, Ridge Road

ELEVATION: 6,000' - 7,785'

GREATEST RELIEF: Cabezón Peak, 1,786'

MAJOR PEAKS: Cabezón Peak (7,785'), Cerro Parido (7,608'), Cerro Cochino (7,072'), Cerro Cuate (7,019')

MAJOR ATTRACTIONS: Mount Taylor, Jémez State Monument, Fenton Lake State Park

HIKING: Continental Divide Trail. Cabezón Peak, hiking and rock climbing but no designated trails.

WINTER ACTIVITIES: None

VEGETATION: Piñon juniper woodland, ponderosa pine, gambel oak, grasses

WILDLIFE: Mule deer, mountain lion, elk, black bear, bobcat, pronghorn, golden eagles

WATER: No surface water.

SEASON: Year round. Approach roads may be impassable after heavy rains due to the clay composition of the soil.

WILDERNESS: Ojito declared wilderness (11,000 acres). Cabezón WSA complex (8,259 acres), Boca del Oso WSA complex (66,401 acres in WSA plus 41,291 additional acres).

ADMINISTRATION: BLM Public Lands

BETWEEN ALBUQUERQUE'S WEST MESA AND MOUNT TAYLOR LIES THE BROAD BASIN OF THE RÍO PUERCO VALLEY, WITH ITS OVERGRAZED GRASSLANDS AND ITS CLUSTERS OF LOW CLIFFS AND BLUFFS IN VARYING SHADES OF SANDSTONE YELLOW.

Standing out from the patchwork of the landscape are the more than fifty dark volcanic plugs, or necks, ringing nearby Mount Taylor. The most prominent is a well-known landmark, Cabezón, the big head. The sheer sides of Cabezón Peak rise more than seventeen hundred feet above the valley floor, to an elevation of 7,785 feet.

Cabezón Peak is a sacred place for the Pueblo Indians and also for the Navajo, who call it *Tse Naajin*, black rock coming down. The Navajo creation story tells how the supernatural Twin Warriors killed an evil giant, cut off his head, and tossed it to the east.

Cabezón Peak and other tall plugs in the area, like Cerro Alesna, have seen a continuing parade of traders, mountain men, gold prospectors, and stagecoaches through the years. The isolated Río Puerco Valley was a haven for rustlers and train robbers, who could find numerous places to hide in the mountain environs. Cole Young, a member of the notorious Black Jack Ketchum gang, held up the Atlantic and Pacific Railroad at the Río Puerco Bridge. A US marshal who happened to be on board the train shot and killed Young.

In the 1870s, several Spanish families settled along the Río Puerco near the base of Cabezón Peak and began sheepherding and farming. The town they called La Posta came to be known as Cabezón in the late 1880s. It was a trading center for the Navajos and other ranchers, with a post office, blacksmith shop, general stores, four or five saloons, and three dance halls. It functioned as a way station for travelers between Santa Fe and the west until the 1940s. Today it is considered one of New Mexico's premier ghost towns, with more than fifteen abandoned buildings, a church, cemetery, and vacant stores. It is located on private property and not open to the general public.

Right: Tse Naajin, *also known as Cabezón Peak (7,785'), is the highest and best-known of the more than fifty volcanic plugs in the Río Puerco Valley. With no walking route to the summit, it presents a challenge to mountaineers.*

Twilight colors the western face of the Sandía Mountains as seen from the Río Grande Bosque near Coronado State Monument, the site where Coronado's expedition wintered in 1540.

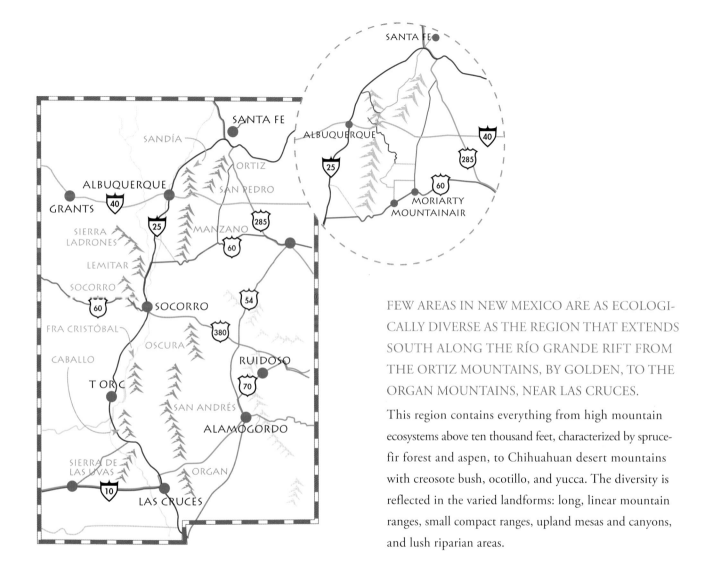

FEW AREAS IN NEW MEXICO ARE AS ECOLOGI-
CALLY DIVERSE AS THE REGION THAT EXTENDS
SOUTH ALONG THE RÍO GRANDE RIFT FROM
THE ORTIZ MOUNTAINS, BY GOLDEN, TO THE
ORGAN MOUNTAINS, NEAR LAS CRUCES.

This region contains everything from high mountain
ecosystems above ten thousand feet, characterized by spruce-
fir forest and aspen, to Chihuahuan desert mountains
with creosote bush, ocotillo, and yucca. The diversity is
reflected in the varied landforms: long, linear mountain
ranges, small compact ranges, upland mesas and canyons,
and lush riparian areas.

The entire central region of the state is defined by the Río Grande and the Río Grande Rift. The river did not cause the rift, it simply flowed, and still flows, in the north-south sequence of linked depressions where the earth's crust subsided as a result of faulting. As the rift sank the land on either side rose, creating the linear, north-south, fault-block mountains that flank the Río Grande. Over the last twenty-five million years, erosion of rift-bordering uplands poured huge volumes of sediment into the chain of basins. The same limestone layers visible at ten thousand feet, on top of the Sandía Mountains, lie beneath ten thousand feet of sediment under the city of Albuquerque.

Typically, the gentle slopes of these central mountains rise to a linear crest and then plunge steeply down an escarpment facing the rift. While the mountain ranges in the south—the San Andrés, Oscura, and Organs—are not as high or as vegetated as the Sandías and Manzanos, they rise dramatically from their low-elevation bases in the desert and have many unique features. There are two designated wilderness areas in the region, the Sandía Wilderness and the Manzano Mountains Wilderness, and several other wilderness study areas further south, including a portion of the spectacular Organ Mountains.

Left: *The Sandía Mountains, bathed in warm storm light, look their wild, rugged best when snow plasters their granite cliffs and clouds conceal the relatively flat summit region.*

ORTIZ & SAN PEDRO MOUNTAINS

LOCATION: Between Madrid and Tijeras

ACCESS: I-40; NM 14, 344

ELEVATION: 5,200' - 8,928'

GREATEST RELIEF: Placer Mountain, 2,416'

MAJOR PEAKS: Ortiz Peak (8,928'), Placer Mountain (8,897'), South Mountain (8,750'), San Pedro Mountain (8,242')

MAJOR ATTRACTIONS: Cerrillos Hills Historic Park, Ortiz Mountains Educational Preserve, Madrid, Cerrillos

HIKING: Limited

WINTER ACTIVITIES: Limited snow sports

VEGETATION: Gambel oak, New Mexico olive, piñon-juniper woodland

WILDLIFE: Porcupine, mule deer, black bear, mountain lion, bobcat, coyote

WATER: Little surface water, intermittent small creeks and springs

SEASON: Year-round

WILDERNESS: No declared wilderness or roadless areas. BLM (South Mountain), private ownership, no access.

ADMINISTRATION: Cíbola National Forest

THE LOW, DOME-SHAPED UPLIFTS BETWEEN MADRID AND TIJERAS JUST EAST OF NM 14, THE TURQUOISE TRAIL NATIONAL SCENIC BYWAY, ARE THE ORTIZ AND SAN PEDRO MOUNTAINS.

These adjoining ranges are mere stumps of their volcanic glory twenty-nine million years ago, when they were more than twice their present height. Wind and water have eroded them to elevations of eight thousand to nine thousand feet. While these mountains do not attract many climbers or hikers, their rich mineral deposits have lured people from near and far for centuries.

Both the Ortiz and the San Pedro Mountains consist of small intrusions that pushed up through the fault zone along the east side of the Río Grande Rift. Among these intrusive rocks were slices of sedimentary and volcanic strata and hot, mineral-rich liquids. One of the most coveted mineral products that originated in those super-heated liquids is turquoise. Turquoise has been mined in

Although overshadowed by the much higher Sandías, the Ortiz and San Pedro Mountains have their own distinctive personality and history.

these mountains and the nearby Cerrillos Hills since 900 AD. Prehistoric inhabitants of the Río Grande Valley used it for ornaments, ceremony, and trade. Turquoise from this area has been found in large quantities in burial sites at Pueblo Bonito in Chaco Canyon and has surfaced as far away as Mexico City and Spain. This is one of the oldest mining districts in North America.

The Spaniards first discovered gold here in the sixteenth century and reportedly used Indian slave labor to mine it. This brutal practice may have been a contributing factor in the Pueblo Revolt of 1680. The mines were hidden after the revolt and not rediscovered until 1828, when a Spanish sheepherder named José Francisco Ortiz discovered gold. Gold was also found near the town of San Pedro in 1832. Those two discoveries reopened the oldest gold mining area in the United States. Other minerals found in these mountains include silver, lead, and zinc.

81

LOCATION: Northeast of Albuquerque

ACCESS: I-40; NM 14, 165, 333; Scenic Byway 536

ELEVATION: 5,500' - 10,678'

GREATEST RELIEF: Sandía Crest, 4,600'

MAJOR PEAKS: Sandía Crest (10,678'), Sandía Peak, (10,447'), South Sandía Peak (9,782')

MAJOR ATTRACTIONS: Sandía Peak Ski Area, Sandía Peak Aerial Tramway, Sandía Crest, Sandía Man Cave, Albuquerque

HIKING: Extensive hiking trails, notably Sandía Crest, La Luz, Pino, Embuditio, Three Gun Spring, Faulty, Cienega

WINTER ACTIVITIES: Scenic Byway NM 536 to Sandía Peak Ski Area and Sandía Crest provides access to some of the best and most accessible cross-country skiing and snowshoeing terrain in New Mexico.

VEGETATION: More than 890 species, including cacti, sage, saltbush, gray oak, piñon-juniper woodland, ponderosa pine, gambel oak, white fir, Douglas fir, limber pine

WILDLIFE: Mule deer, bobcat, black bear, badger, porcupine, mountain lion

WATER: Las Huertas Canyon. Domingo Baca, Embudito, Cienega Canyon (seasonal), Three Gun Spring, Osha Spring, South Sandía Spring, Pino Canyon Spring

SEASON: Year-round

WILDERNESS: Sandía Mountain Wilderness Area (37,232 acres). The Sandía Game Refuge encompasses the entire range. Joint use by Sandía Pueblo and the US Forest Service prevents any new development on the west face.

ADMINISTRATION: Cíbola National Forest, Sandía Ranger District

Opposite: *A view down the rugged west face of the Sandía Mountains near Sandía Crest (10,678') reveals their great vertical relief.*

THE RUGGED, OFTEN-PINKISH WEST FACE OF THE SANDÍA MOUNTAINS DOMINATES ALBUQUERQUE'S SKYLINE AND FORMS A NATURAL EASTERN BOUNDARY FOR THE CITY.

Rising to 10,678 feet at Sandía Crest, the range encompasses more than four hundred square miles and contains mixtures of the lush and the arid, the wild and the developed. Sandía, the Spanish word for watermelon, may refer to the watermelon-colored granite face of the mountains at sunset or possibly to the large gourds that grow at the nearby pueblo, which early Spanish explorers confused with watermelons. In the Tiwa language of the Isleta and Sandía Pueblos, the mountain is called *Oku Pin*, turtle mountain. In the related Tewa language, it is referred to as *Bien Mur*, big mountain.

The Sandía Mountains were formed five to ten million years ago, when a massive block of the earth's crust tilted up and sideways. The fault block consists of 1.4-billion-year-old Precambrian granite topped with 300-million-year-old Pennsylvanian rocks that were formed from ocean sediments. The huge face of granite that dominates the northern profile of the mountains, sometimes referred to as the shield, was formed from cooling magma. The same kinds of sedimentary rocks that are on the top of the mountains can be found, a few miles away, buried nearly twenty thousand feet below the Río Grande. The impressive relief of these mountains is emphasized by the even greater depth of the Río Grande Rift. Adding the depth of the rift to the five-thousand-foot rise of the mountains above Albuquerque indicates that the total fault movement was approximately five miles. Over time, the steep, craggy western slope of the Sandías has been ornately sculpted by erosion.

Some of the earliest inhabitants of North America lived in the Sandía Mountains ten to twenty thousand years ago. The climate was cooler and more humid than it is today, and large mammals such as camels and great bison roamed the foothills. A large group of ancient people inhabited what is now Las Huertas Canyon. Although no physical remains have been found, they left behind flint tools and charcoal from their fires. By dating that charcoal and the bones of long-extinct animals, archaeologists have theorized that very early Puebloan people occupied this region. The Sandía Mountains area continued to be inhabited by nomadic groups for the next several thousand years. Archaic people relied more on small animals and wild plants than their predecessors. Then larger, more permanent communities practiced agriculture and made pottery. These were the ancestors of today's Pueblo Indians, who settled in and built their multistoried communities, or pueblos, with central plazas and kivas. Spanish explorers who ventured up the Río Grande in 1540 documented twenty pueblos in the Albuquerque vicinity.

The first Spanish expedition, led by Don Francisco Vázquez de Coronado, spent the winter of 1540-41 in the pueblo of Kuaua, on the west bank of the Río Grande across from what is now Bernalillo. Other expeditions followed, including the one led by Don Juan de Oñate. The Spaniards established missions in the larger pueblos and attempted to convert the native peoples, often against their will. In 1680 the pueblos rose in rebellion, and the Spaniards were expelled for twelve years. In 1692, the Spaniards returned and established new settlements, including Alburquerque (the first "r" was later dropped), in 1706, and Carnuel, a small settlement in Tijeras Canyon in the Sandías. Confederate troops camped in Tijeras Canyon during the Civil War, and Dust Bowl refugees during the Great Depression established camps in the mountains on their way to California. During the 1930s, the Civilian Conservation Corp constructed Juan Tabo and La Cueva Campgrounds in the Sandía Mountains.

From the left: The Shield, the Needle and the distinctive aguille called the Thumb in the North Sandía Mountains, as seen from the banks of the Río Grande.

A Perfect Hike

After thirty-five years of tramping the mountains and forests of the American West, I can recall numerous hikes with fondness. On a trip through Wyoming's Wind River Range, we used llamas and carried only token packs so we could penetrate deep into the wilderness. The spectacular landscape of granite peaks, the upland lakes and meadows and the sheer vastness of the wilderness made that trip unforgettable.

One of the best hikes I have taken was in the Weminuche Wilderness in Southwestern Colorado. The Grenadier-Needle High Route, mostly off trail and above timberline, crosses five passes that are over twelve thousand feet and climaxes with the view of the three 14er's surrounding Twin Lakes.

I remember many fine hikes into the Wheeler Peak Wilderness or the Pecos Wilderness high country, sometimes with friends, sometimes alone. Some were to timberline or a summit, some just long walks through the densely wooded forests. The annual pilgrimage to Santa Fe Baldy is always much anticipated. The long hike is rewarded with a cold beverage at the end of the trail and often followed by fine New Mexican grub at a Santa Fe restaurant—a fantastic way to cap a fine day of mountain tramping.

Great as these hikes are, my perfect hike is quite a bit closer to home. It begins with a hot cup of coffee on my back deck, relaxing with my wife Sue while we wait for our friends. When we take to the trail, we head out the backyard gate and follow a beaten path until, in a few minutes, we pick up the main trail. On a one-and-a-half mile ascending traverse through the upper Sonoran Zone, we cross seasonal streams and appreciate an ever-changing panorama of the ramparts we are to soon ascend. A turn on the shoulder of a lower canyon brings the main trail into view, coming up on a south-facing slope. People are slowly hiking up the switchbacks in the sun that has now just breached the highest ridges of the mountain. We are on a north-facing slope, and so enjoy shade and a much cooler hike while on the lower reaches. A nice three-quarter-mile hike puts us at an inspirational overlook and ends the first third of the hike.

The second stage of the hike brings us into the transitional zone, dominated by ponderosa pine. The views of the upper canyon we are soon to enter get better with each step. The higher we hike, the more defined the canyon we are in becomes. The views to the west become narrower as the first band of rock walls start to encroach. We continue past an awesome spire called The Thumb, turn a sharp switchback and abruptly enter a world of aspen, conifer, and talus slopes. Remnants of the great walls of granite close in; the weathering of the ages is evident all around us. Our world becomes more intimate the higher we ascend. The western expanse is now cut off by granite spires, aguilles and precipitous cliff faces. Great walls loom to our left, a playground for rock climbers—the conquistadors of the useless.* My heart quickens, as much at the views that surround us as for the elevation. We are now well into the Canadian Zone and around nine thousand feet in elevation. The forest cover, north slope position, and higher elevation, along with more humidity, keep the ambient temperature a balmy fifty degrees, perfect for hiking. By now the desert floor, where we started our hike in, is rapidly approaching eighty degrees, far too hot for a perfect hike. If it is too early in the season, patches of snow impede our progress. The snow always takes us by surprise, as the view of the mountain has been free of snow for a few months.

Just when we think that perhaps we should have waited until a little later in the season, the landscape changes again. Gone are the granite spires, the claustrophobic canyon and the snow. Stratified limestone, scrub oak, aspen, and increas-ingly expansive views signal the last third of the hike. We are now over ten thousand feet and have entered the Hudsonian Zone, our companion for the remainder of the hike. We know we are close and our pace quickens a bit. A fork in the trail tells us we are near the top. An easing of the grade and a southern exposure urges us along. Increasing traffic coming down the trail tells us we are very near. We arrive at the summit house, an elevation of 10,478 feet. If we have done the hike right it is now noon, the temperature is still fifty degrees, and the Summit House is now serving cold brews.

Where is there such a hike? Of course, it is the La Luz Trail, on the west side of the Sandía Mountains. This annual hike heralds the start of the hiking season, tells me I can still "make the grade," and gives me a chance to share the experience with my friends. I can start at my doorstep, hike ten miles through a spectacular ever-changing landscape, gain over four thousand feet in elevation, top out in a sub-alpine landscape, and know there is a cold brew waiting for me at the top to reward my exertions and a tram ride down to save my knees. If that isn't perfect, I don't know what is.

Mike Butterfield

*From the title of mountaineer Lionel Terray's memoirs.

LOCATION: East of Belén and Los Lunas

ACCESS: US 60; NM 337, 55, 47; Forest Roads 422, 33

ELEVATION: 5,700' - 10,098'

GREATEST RELIEF: Manzano Peak, 3,900'

MAJOR PEAKS: Manzano Peak (10,098'), Gallo Peak (10,003'), Bosque Peak (9,610'), Mosca Peak (9,509'), Guadalupe Peak (9,450'), Capilla Peak (9,375')

MAJOR ATTRACTIONS: Salinas Pueblo Missions National Monument, Manzano Mountains State Park

HIKING: Fourth of July Canyon, Trigo Canyon, Manzano Peak, Comanche Canyon, Manzano Crest Trail

WINTER ACTIVITIES: Some cross-country skiing in Fourth of July Canyon. Access might be muddy.

VEGETATION: Piñon-juniper woodland, ponderosa pine, alligator juniper, spruce, fir, aspen, desert scrub

WILDLIFE: Important raptor flyway; mountain lion, deer, desert bighorn sheep

WATER: Fourth of July Canyon, Red Canyon (seasonal), Spruce Spring, Ox Springs, Trigo Springs, New Canyon Springs. Very little permanent surface water; bring your own water.

SEASON: April in lower elevations, mid-May for upper reaches. Snow generally blankets the area December through March.

WILDERNESS: Manzano Mountains Wilderness (36,970 acres)

ADMINISTRATION: Cíbola National Forest, Sandía Ranger District

Opposite: *The twin summits of Guadalupe Peak (9,450'), left, and Mosca Peak (9,509') anchor the north end of the Manzano Mountains. Larger in area and nearly as high as the Sandías, these mountains get little attention despite their proximity to New Mexico's largest urban area.*

THE UNDERRATED MANZANO MOUNTAIN RANGE, JUST SOUTH OF THE SANDÍA MOUNTAINS, IS BIGGER AND WILDER THAN ITS BETTER-KNOWN SISTER RANGE AND HAS PLENTY OF MYSTERY AND UNIQUE FEATURES.

After all, the Manzanos contain the Fourth of July Canyon, with its fall foliage display, the John F. Kennedy Campground, a 37,000-acre wilderness area, and possibly a lost silver mine concealed by Indians after the 1680 Pueblo Revolt. The Manzanos extend for forty miles; the Sandías are only twenty-eight miles long. The Manzanos are more challenging to access, though. The entire northern part of the range is closed to the public by Isleta Pueblo and Kirtland Air Force Base landholdings.

Like the Sandías, the Manzano Mountains are a tilted block of ancient Precambrian granite topped by east-dipping Pennsylvanian limestone. Here, as elsewhere in the vicinity, the Río Grande Rift is much deeper than it looks. Since forming about twenty-five million years ago, its chain of basins has filled with thousands of feet of lake sediments and alluvium, some of which predate the formation of the Río Grande drainage. The river valley here is thirty miles wide, by far the largest of the sediment-filled basins along the rift.

The inhabitants of nearby Isleta Pueblo believe their people originally lived at the base of the Manzano Mountains, to the east of their present pueblo on the Río Grande. In the 1600s, the Spanish found several thriving Puebloan trade communities in the Manzano foothills and established missions there. By the 1870s the entire Salinas district, as the Spanish had renamed it, was largely abandoned by both Spaniards and Native Americans. All that now remains are the ruins of four mission churches and the partially excavated pueblo of Gran Quivira, formerly known as Las Humanas. Some of the ruins can still be seen at the Abo, Quarai, and Gran Quivira units at Salinas Pueblo Missions National Monument.

Manzano is Spanish for apple; the mountains were named after the apple orchards planted around the village of Manzano in 1800. The few trees remaining there are probably some of the oldest apple trees in the country. Some of the early Hispanic villages in the Manzanos are still occupied. The wild lands of the Manzano Mountains Wilderness exist essentially as they have for centuries.

The spectacular fall foliage display in Fourth of July Canyon in the Manzano Mountains is highly anticipated. It is one of the few places in New Mexico where big tooth maple grow and perhaps the best-known, most visited area in the entire Manzano range.

LOCATION: West of I-25 near Bernardo, County Road B12

ACCESS: I-25 Bernardo Exit; County Road B12

ELEVATION: 5,200' - 9,210'

GREATEST RELIEF: Ladrón Peak, 3,450'

MAJOR PEAKS: Ladrón Peak (East Summit) (9,176'), Monte Negro (7,581')

MAJOR ATTRACTIONS: Salinas Pueblo Missions National Monument

HIKING: Limited, due to lack of trails and rugged terrain.

VEGETATION: Piñon-juniper woodland, ponderosa pine, Douglas fir, desert scrub

WILDLIFE: Black bear, mountain lion, mule deer, pronghorn, and reintroduction area for desert bighorn sheep

WATER: Río Salado Watershed

SEASON: Spring and fall are best.

WINTER ACTIVITIES: Limited snow sports

WILDERNESS: Sierra Ladrones Wilderness Study Area (45,308 acres plus 54,936 acres additional roadless area), Sevilleta National Wildlife Refuge

ADMINISTRATION: BLM, US Fish and Wildlife Service, private

THE SMALL, ISOLATED, RUGGED SIERRA LADRONES ARE CHARACTERIZED BY ROCKY CLIFFS, STEEP SLOPES, AND BADLANDS CUT BY NUMEROUS RAVINES.

The Río Salado drains the south side of the Ladrones and runs through the precipitous walls of the Salado Box, sometimes referred to as a mini-Grand Canyon.

The Sierra Ladrones exhibit remarkable geologic diversity, with uplifted three-million-year-old volcanic lava flows, fossil-laden limestone over 300 million years old, and Precambrian granite over 600 million years old at the core. Anyone fortunate enough to make the summit will face the challenge of hiking around house-size boulders. For geology buffs, the area contains the northernmost known exposures of Lower Mississippian rocks in New Mexico, dating from 220 million years ago.

The rugged massif of Sierra Ladrón, reflected in an ephemeral melt pond at twilight, presents its subtle side.

In combination with the adjacent Sevilleta National Wildlife Refuge, the area contains habitat for almost two hundred wildlife species and a great diversity of plants. It is notable as a site for the reintroduction of desert bighorn sheep and for critical raptor wintering and nesting areas. In a broader context, the Sierra Ladrones are an essential biological link between the Bear Mountains to the west and the Manzano Mountains to the east. A 36,000-acre portion of the Sierra Ladrones has been designated a wilderness study area.

Sierra Ladrones is Spanish for thieves' mountains. During Spanish colonial times, Navajo and Apache raiding parties would retreat to these mountains with livestock stolen from villages along the Río Grande. Later, Hispanic and Anglo rustlers and thieves used the many steep-sided, treacherous canyons for hideouts and ambush. Some gold was found in these mountains in the late 1860s.

LOCATION: West of Socorro

ACCESS: I-25; US 60

ELEVATION: 4,600' - 7,292'

GREATEST RELIEF: Socorro Peak, 2,600'

MAJOR PEAKS: Lemitar Mountains: Polvadera Mountain (7,292') and Strawberrry Peak (7,012'), Socorro Mountains: Socorro Peak (7,243')

MAJOR ATTRACTIONS: Bosque del Apache National Wildlife Refuge, Sevilleta National Wildlife Refuge, El Camino Real, San Lorenzo Canyon.

HIKING: Strawberry Peak; rock climbing at Box Canyon

WINTER ACTIVITIES: Limited snow sports

VEGETATION: Piñon-juniper woodland, oak, desert scrub

WILDLIFE: Pronghorn, mountain lion, mule deer, black bear

WATER: No surface water

SEASON: Year-round

WILDERNESS: No declared wilderness, WSA or roadless areas. Sevilleta National Wildlife Refuge abuts the northern boundary of the mountains.

ADMINISTRATION: Bureau of Land Management

THE SOCORRO AND LEMITAR MOUNTAINS ARE FAULT–BLOCK MOUNTAINS, NARROW, LOW-LYING AND NEARLY BARREN.

Their western slopes are composed primarily of volcanic rock formed by lava flows, lava domes, and large quantities of tuff. The many basinlike calderas are the remains of collapsed volcanoes. The Socorro Mountains, along with the Sierra Ladrones, have the distinction of being the earthquake center of New Mexico. Earthquakes have been observed in the region since 1855 but probably occurred well before that date. A seismograph station at the base of Socorro Peak generally records two or three weak quakes a day. The high frequency of small quakes may prevent

Socorro Peak (7,243'), known primarily as a backdrop to the town of Socorro, has a rugged nature and great local relief. It is easily identified by the large "M" near its summit, placed there by the New Mexico School of Mines.

the accumulation of pressure that otherwise might lead to a significant quake.

Socorro Peak is easily recognizable from the highway by the letter "M" near the top. It is the site of the New Mexico School of Mines, founded by the state in 1893 to train mining engineers. Now called the New Mexico Institute of Mining Technology, it maintains geophysical laboratories on the mountain, so access is restricted. The Lemitar Mountains are the northern extension of the Socorro Mountains and have two named summits, Polvadera Mountain and Strawberry Peak.

Archaeological evidence indicates that people from the prehistoric Folsom, Cochise, Basketmaker, and Pueblo cultures were in the Socorro/Lemitar Mountain region. Tools made from the mountains' jasper and chalcedony have been found in the area. The Piro Indians, who lived along the Río Grande here until Spanish times, left during the Pueblo Revolt of 1680. The region was resettled by Spanish families under a land grant in 1817. Silver was discovered in 1867, and Socorro became the largest city in New Mexico during the mining boom in 1890. The Socorro Mountain mines alone yielded $1 million worth of silver.

SAN ANDRÉS & OSCURA MOUNTAINS

The closest most people get to the San Andrés Mountains is the view from White Sands National Monument in the Tularosa Valley. This range is on a military reservation and is closed to the public.

LOCATION: Between the Tularosa Valley and the Jornada del Muerto.

ACCESS: White Sands Missile Range, no public access

ELEVATION: 4,558' - 8,958'

GREATEST RELIEF: Salinas Peak, 4,281'

MAJOR PEAKS: San Andrés Mountains: Salinas Peak (8,958'), San Andrés Peak (8,241'), San Agustín Peak (7,030')

Oscura Mountains: Oscura Peak (8,732') and North Oscura Peak (7,999')

MAJOR ATTRACTIONS: White Sands National Monument, Trinity Site

HIKING: Not open to the public without permission from White Sands Missile Range.

WINTER ACTIVITIES: Not open to the public. Limited snow sports.

VEGETATION: Grasses, piñon-juniper woodland, creosote, yucca, prickly pear

WILDLIFE: Desert bighorn sheep, mule deer, mountain lion

WATER: No surface water

SEASON: Year-round

WILDERNESS: San Andrés Mountains roadless areas: south (240,000 acres), central (155,000 acres), and north (150,000 acres). San Andrés Wildlife Refuge.

ADMINISTRATION: White Sands Missile Range, US Fish and Wildlife Service

---

THE SAN ANDRÉS AND OSCURA MOUNTAINS ARE DRY, BARREN RANGES THAT RUN PARALLEL TO THE RÍO GRANDE AND LIE ALMOST ENTIRELY WITHIN THE WHITE SANDS MISSILE RANGE.

Trinity Site, where the first nuclear explosion took place, lies between these two ranges.

The San Andrés Mountains, named by Spanish missionaries after the disciple St. Andrew, are considered the best and largest desert bighorn sheep habitat in New Mexico and one of the least-disturbed natural areas in the state. The US Army, the US Fish and Wildlife Service, and the New Mexico Department of Game and Fish have been involved in an ongoing effort to reintroduce and help recover the desert bighorn sheep in the San Andrés National Wildlife Refuge. The San Andrés range has maintained its wilderness character and is an important corridor for the movement of other wildlife, including mule deer and mountain lion.

Paleoindian sites in the foothills of the San Andrés Mountains indicate that this area was occupied in prehistoric times. Attracted to the springs and natural resources, prehistoric and, later, Puebloan groups occupied the San Andrés and the basin between the ranges. The San Andrés are also a significant part of the Apache traditional-use area.

The San Andrés Mountains lie next to the vast parched area aptly named the Jornada del Muerto—the journey of the dead man. Spanish explorers routinely died of thirst trying to cross the Jornada, which lies in the rain shadows for storms passing east or west. According to legend, there is a lost gold mine on Soledad Peak. It was discovered by Padre La Rue and allegedly hidden and sealed when Spanish soldiers approached. The secret of its exact location died when the padre was murdered.

Geologically similar to the San Andrés Mountains and separated only by Mockingbird Gap, the Oscura Mountains are a southern extension of the Chupadera Hills.

The name Oscura, which means dark, likely refers to the mountains' relatively dark appearance as a result of volcanic rocks and vegetation near the top of the range. This darkness is especially striking in contrast to the barren gray summits of the San Andrés Mountains. The Oscuras have a rugged western fault scarp and a more gentle eastern slope, just the reverse of the San Andrés Mountains whose steep fault scarp is on the east side. Both ranges have thick layers of sedimentary rocks resting on ancient igneous and metamorphic rocks. These two mountain ranges were lifted during the development of the Río Grand Rift about thirty million years ago. Crustal faulting at that time also dropped two of New Mexico's prominent basins: the Jornada del Muerto to the west and the Tularosa Basin to the east. Together, these two arid basins constitute one of the greatest biogeographic barriers to the east-west movement of animals in the Southwest.

Opposite: *Another view of the San Andrés Mountains west of White Sands National Monument.*

FRA CRISTÓBAL & CABALLO MOUNTAINS

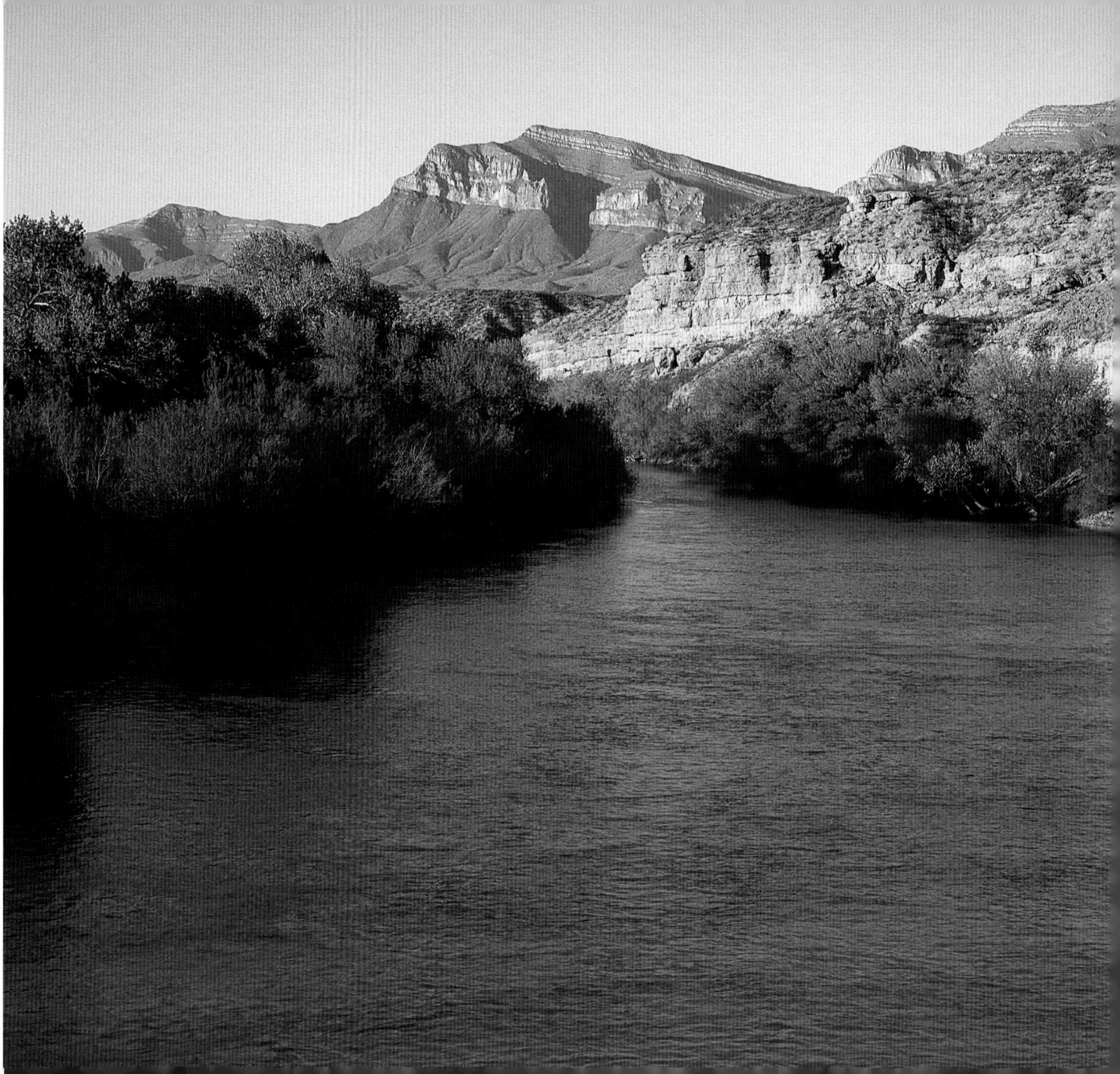

LOCATION: East of the Río Grande, between Elephant Butte Lake State Park and Hatch

ACCESS: I-25 Hatch Exit #41; NM 51; improved dirt roads

ELEVATION: Fra Cristóbal Mountains, 4,400' - 6,834'; Caballo Mountains, 4,200' - 7,565'

GREATEST RELIEF: Fra Cristóbal Mountains: Unnamed peak, 2,434'
Caballo Mountains: Timber Mountain, 3,365'

MAJOR PEAKS: Fra Cristóbal Mountains: Fra Cristóbal Mountain (6,003')
Caballo Mountains: Brushy Mountain (7,375'), Timber Mountain (7,300')

MAJOR ATTRACTIONS: Elephant Butte Lake, Caballo Lake, and Percha Dam State Parks

HIKING: No designated trails. Old roads and tracks can be hiked in the Caballo Mountains.

WINTER ACTIVITIES: No snow activities

VEGETATION: Grasses, piñon-juniper woodland, creosote, yucca, wide variety of cacti, some with special status

WILDLIFE: Mule deer, mountain lion, bobcat, nesting raptors, bats, excellent potential reintroduction site for desert bighorn sheep

WATER: No surface water. Caballo Lake is nearby.

SEASON: Fall, winter, and spring are best.

WILDERNESS: Caballo Mountains Wilderness Inventory Unit (28,800 acres)

ADMINISTRATION: Pedro Armendaris Land Grant in the Fra Cristobals, Bureau of Land Management and state lands in the Caballos

Left: *The Caballo Mountains are the highest and wildest range in the nearly unbroken chain of mountains bordering the Río Grande on the east.*

THE FRA CRISTÓBAL AND CABALLO MOUNTAINS, AN ALMOST CONTINUOUS BARE MOUNTAIN CHAIN ON THE EAST SIDE OF THE RÍO GRANDE, MARK A LINE OF FORMER UPLIFT ALONG THE RÍO GRANDE RIFT.

The twenty-mile-long Fra Cristóbal Range rises to an elevation of 6,003 feet at Fra Cristóbal Mountain, the named peak of the range. The entire range lies within the boundaries of the Pedro Armendaris Land Grant and Ranch. Some ancient granite is visible at the foot of the western face of the mountains, but most of the face consists of Magdalena limestone. On the eastern slope are several large limestone caves with millions of bats. The well-known hot springs at Truth or Consequences rise along the faults at the edge of these mountains.

The Fra Cristóbal range provides a home for a reintroduced population of desert bighorn sheep managed by the Ted Turner Endangered Species Fund. Other large mammals in the mountains and on the nearby ranch include pronghorn, mule deer, mountain lion, and African oryx.

The Caballo Mountains, just south of the Fra Cristóbals, overlook Caballo Lake. The steep, rugged western escarpment is composed of contorted fault block with dramatic limestone cliffs and spires. The eastern slopes are gentler, gradually flattening into the Jornada del Muerto. The highly variable geology and elevations of these mountains make this a true sky island, with a great diversity of habitats and plant communities. The area in and around the Caballo Mountains is known by geologists as a place where almost the entire geologic history of New Mexico is exposed at the land surface. For example, billion-year-old granites that form the geologic basement for much of North America are visible at the western base of the Caballos. Just above that, a dramatic break in the color and form of rock represents the first widespread seas and the earliest marine sedimentary strata.

The Caballo Mountains are divided by a pass in the middle of the range called Palomas Gap, named for the doves in the cottonwoods along the river. North Ridge, the divide north of the Gap, has one major summit, Caballo Cone. Timber Mountain, at South Ridge, is the range's highest point at 7,300 feet. These mountains have been recommended by the New Mexico Wilderness Alliance as a wilderness inventory unit, but past and proposed mining activities may keep them from acquiring wilderness status.

LOCATION: South of Hatch

ACCESS: I-25; NM 26, 185; County Roads C9, D12

ELEVATION: 4,800' - 6,625'

GREATEST RELIEF: Magdalena Peak, 1,760'

MAJOR PEAKS: Magdalena Peak (6,625'), Tailholt Mountain (6,027')

MAJOR ATTRACTIONS: Leasburg Dam and Rockhound State Parks

HIKING: No designated trails, but open terrain for hiking

WINTER ACTIVITIES: No snow activities

VEGETATION: Grasses, piñon-juniper woodland, velvet ash, netleaf hackberry, desert willow

WILDLIFE: Pronghorn, mule deer, mountain lion, bobcat, nesting raptors, golden and bald eagles

WATER: No surface water; intermittent streams

SEASON: Spring, fall

WILDERNESS: No declared wilderness. Robledo Mountains and Las Uvas Mountains Wilderness Study Unit (combined 23,563 acres), roadless area (186,437 acres)

ADMINISTRATION: Bureau of Land Management, state lands

THE SIERRA DE LAS UVAS, MOUNTAINS OF GRAPES, IS A SMALLISH, ARID RANGE THAT DOESN'T SEEM TO LIVE UP TO ITS NAME.

The only apparent source of grapes is a single common canyon vine at the extreme north end of the range. Closer examination reveals that this range does have some assets. It has a real wilderness feel, and it contains a diverse range of landscape forms and habitat types, including juniper-dotted volcanic mountains, dramatic limestone cliffs, remote grass-covered hills, mesas, buttes, caves, and rugged box canyons.

Elevations in the area range from about four thousand feet to more than six thousand feet on Magdalena Peak. With so much variation in habitat and elevation, there is an exceptional diversity of vegetation and wildlife. Of special note are the black grama grasslands on the mesas and the arroyo riparian areas with plants like velvet ash, netleaf hackberry, and desert willow.

The Sierra de las Uvas also provide habitat for rare birds like the Aplomado falcon and Baird's sparrow, the endangered peregrine falcon, and an abundance of raptors and unusual reptiles. There is evidence of prehistoric habitation in the form of pithouse villages and outstanding petroglyph sites. In more recent history, stagecoaches carried mail through this area on the Butterfield Trail.

SIERRA DE LAS UVAS

LOCATION: East of Las Cruces

ACCESS: I-25; US 70/82; County Road 17, Dripping Springs Road

ELEVATION: 4,000' - 9,012'

GREATEST RELIEF: Organ Needle, 4,338'

MAJOR PEAKS: Organ Needle (9,012'), Organ Peak (8,870'), Granite Peak (8,731'), Rabbit Ear Plateau (8,150'), Baylor Peak (7,721')

MAJOR ATTRACTIONS: Dripping Springs and Aguirre Springs Recreation Areas, Leasburg Dam State Park, Fort Selden State Monument, Mesilla Valley Bosque State Park.

HIKING: Aguirre Springs, Ice Canyon, Pine Tree, Fillmore Canyon Trail to Organ Peak summit, Baylor Pass

WINTER ACTIVITIES: No snow activities

VEGETATION: Grasses, piñon-juniper woodland, ponderosa pine, mountain mahogany, oaks, mesquite

WILDLIFE: Mule deer, mountain lion, bobcat, golden eagles, hawks, owls, peregrine falcons, Organ Mountains race of Colorado chipmunk (special status), four species of endemic mollusks

WATER: Dripping Springs on the west side. Usually, there is a reliable stream on the east side along the Pine Tree Trail.

SEASON: Year-round, weather permitting. Spring and fall are best. Summer can be hot.

WILDERNESS: Organ Mountains Wilderness Study Area (7,283'), additional 57,709-acres roadless area

ADMINISTRATION: Bureau of Land Management, private holdings, state lands

ORGAN MOUNTAINS

Left: One of the most spectacular ranges in New Mexico, the Organ Mountains near Las Cruces are a rock climber's paradise. This view includes the distinctive Rabbit Ears (8,150') and the higher, crenulated crest south to Organ Needle (9,012'), the range's highest peak.

THE ORGAN MOUNTAINS, WHICH PROVIDE A DRAMATIC BACKDROP FOR LAS CRUCES, ARE AMONG THE STEEPEST, MOST RUGGED MOUNTAIN RANGES IN THE UNITED STATES AND ONE OF THE PREMIER ROCK CLIMBING AREAS IN NEW MEXICO.

These towering peaks are named for the needlelike spires that resemble the pipes of an organ. The principal features of the Organs are related to formation of the Río Grande Rift. About thirty-five million years ago, volcanic eruptions on an uplifted, rift-edge block produced a two-mile-thick column of ash falls that welded together before being eroded into the towers we see today. The Organ Mountains encompass extremely rugged terrain, with a multitude of steep-sided canyons, blocky rock outcrops, red rhyolite cliffs, and white ridges of volcanic tuff.

Archaeological evidence indicates that the Organ Mountains were inhabited by prehistoric people as long as seven thousand years ago. A significant number of artifacts have been uncovered in La Cueva and the Peña Blanca rock shelters. In more recent history, the hermit of Hermit's Peak fame, Giovanni Augustino, met his demise in an Organ Mountain cave, by an Apache lance, in 1867.

Mining activity in the Organ Mountains started in 1854 and reached boom proportions between 1881 and 1906. The village of Organ was the largest mining camp near the well-known Torpedo Mine, which produced copper in 1907.

The Organ Mountains district yielded some $2.5 million worth of copper, lead, silver, gold, and zinc ores during its heyday.

The Wheeler survey expedition came through the region in the 1870s and described the Organs as lofty, rugged, and inaccessible. The first recorded ascent of the highest summit, Organ Needle, was made in 1904. Climbing has remained extremely popular in the Organs despite the hazards—loose rock, rattlesnakes, thorny plants, and extreme heat. Climbers are attracted to the fascinating array of needles, towers, walls, and high-angled faces.

The Organ Mountains provide outstanding recreational opportunities, including hiking on national recreation area trails, backpacking, horseback riding, birding, and nature photography. The range contains the Organ Mountains Wilderness Study Area, the Organ Needles Wilderness Study Area, Aguirre Springs and Dripping Springs National Recreation Areas, and a scenic area of critical environmental concern that is designated to protect the natural and cultural resources in the range.

This view from the aptly named Pine Tree Trail above the Aguirre Springs National Recreation Area, on the east side of the Organ Mountains, reveals not only these mountains' rugged character but vegetation that is unexpectedly lush for such a high, rough desert range.

From the great massif of Carrizo Mountain (9,605'), the Jicarilla Mountains run north and the Capitán Mountains due east. The relatively young lava flow in the mid-ground of this photo, in Valley of Fires Recreation Area, originated from Little Black Peak.

THE LANDSCAPE OF SOUTHEASTERN NEW MEXICO IS PREDOMINANTLY VAST DRY PLAINS WITH WIDELY SPACED CHIHUAHUAN DESERT SHRUBS AND GRASSES.

The few lofty mountain ranges to the west create welcome relief and stand out in great contrast to their flat surroundings. Ironically, these hot, arid mountain ranges and the deep caves they contain owe their existence and their unique character to the force of water.

About 250 million years ago, during the Permian Period, the shallow waters of an ancient sea covered this entire region. Great reefs formed in the waters and, over time, were buried by younger sediments and compressed into limestone. Later, as the earth's crust moved and shifted, these compressed reefs were uplifted and exhumed by erosion to become the rugged, dramatic mountains we see today. These reef mountains are characterized by long, high ridges flanked by steep-sided canyons, and they contain spectacular caves such as Carlsbad Caverns and Lechuguilla Cave.

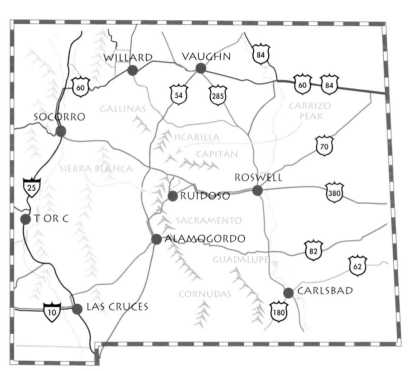

LOCATION: West of Corona
ACCESS: US Highways 60, 54; Forest Road 99
ELEVATION: 7,000' - 8,615'
GREATEST RELIEF: Gallinas Peak , 1,906'
MAJOR PEAKS: Gallinas Peak, (8,615'),
Rough Mountain (8,525')
MAJOR ATTRACTIONS: Cíbola National Forest,
Salinas and Abó National Monuments
HIKING: No designated trails
WINTER ACTIVITIES: Limited snow cover and a
long approach preclude any serious winter activities.
VEGETATION: Piñon-juniper woodland, creosote,
cacti, desert willow
WILDLIFE: Elk, mule deer, turkey, black bear, badger,
bobcat, porcupine
WATER: No surface water
SEASON: Spring through fall
WILDERNESS: No WSA or declared wilderness areas.
Part of Cíbola National Forest.
ADMINISTRATION: Cíbola National Forest

THE GALLINAS MOUNTAINS IN SOUTHEAST-ERN NEW MEXICO ARE A SMALL, ISOLATED RANGE DIRECTLY WEST OF CORONA.

Gallinas, the Spanish word for hens, chickens, and wild turkeys, is a popular name for mountains in this state, probably because the wild birds were abundant in these rugged areas.

There is another Gallinas Range northwest of Magdalena, and there are at least three different Gallina or Gallinas Peaks.

The southeastern Gallinas Mountains consist of several rounded rocky outcrops formed by the intrusion of granite into Permian Period rocks. Halka Chronic, in *Roadside Geology of New Mexico,* describes them as "the Loch Ness monster surfacing through the waves of juniper trees." Gallinas Peak is the highest point and the main drainage is Redcloud Canyon on the southwest side.

At one time there was a mining town called Redcloud in the canyon. Iron and fluorite copper were mined there in the late nineteenth and early twentieth centuries. Today, a US Forest Service campground is at the site.

THE JICARILLAS, THE NORTHERNMOST
MOUNTAINS IN THE SACRAMENTO RANGE,
RISE TO AN ALTITUDE OF NEARLY 7,900 FEET.

They were named after the nomadic Jicarilla Apaches, who probably came here in search of game. These mountains are rich in minerals. Cowboys found placer gold in a gulch nearby in 1850, and in the years that followed some $90,000 worth of gold was mined. Attempts have been made to exploit the abundant gypsum and clay deposits, but currently there is no mining activity. The lack of water makes mining impractical.

Nearby, but not part of the Jicarillas, are three isolated massifs: Patos Mountain (8,508'), Carrizo Mountain (9,605'), and Vera Cruz Mountain (7,801'). Patos Mountain is accessible from an old wagon road between White Oaks and Phillips Ranch and from the base trail on the north side of the mountain. Patos Lake, now usually dry, once held abundant water and attracted wild ducks—*patos* in Spanish. Carrizo Mountain can be climbed via the four-mile Johnnie Canyon Trail on the southeast side or the five-and-a- half mile Water Canyon Trail from White Oaks.

Vera Cruz Mountain, in what are sometimes known as the Tucson Mountains, was named for an 1880s gold mine. The ore from the Vera Cruz proved to be low-grade, so the mine and camp faded quickly.

LOCATION: Eight miles southeast of Ancho
ACCESS: US 54, 380; NM 349
MAJOR PEAKS: Lone Mountain (8,145'), Ancho Peak (7,825'), Jicarilla Peak (7,688'), Jack's Peak (7,553')
ELEVATION: 5,800' - 8,145'
GREATEST RELIEF: Lone Mountain, 2375'
MAJOR ATTRACTIONS: White Oaks (ghost town), Valley of Fires (Malpais)
HIKING: No designated trails in the Jicarilla Mountains. Nearby are the Tucson Trail on Tucson Mountain and the Johnnie Canyon Trail on Carrizo Mountain.
WINTER ACTIVITIES: Limited snow cover
VEGETATION: Piñon-juniper woodland, ponderosa pine, Arizona ash, netleaf hackberry
WILDLIFE: Elk, mule deer, turkey, black bear, badger, bobcat, porcupine
WATER: No surface water in the Jicarillas. Goat spring on nearby Tucson Mountain.
SEASON: April through November
WILDERNESS: No declared wilderness areas
ADMINISTRATION: Lincoln National Forest

JICARILLA MOUNTAINS

LOCATION: East of Carizzozo and north of Capitán

ACCESS: US 380; NM 246 (from the north), 368 (from the east); Forest Roads 338, 56, 616, 57

ELEVATION: 5,700' - 10,201'

GREATEST RELIEF: Capitán Peak, 3,870'

MAJOR PEAKS: Palko Peak (10,201'), Capitán Peak (10,083), Sunset Peak (9,320)

MAJOR ATTRACTIONS: Smokey Bear Historical Park, Lincoln State Monument, Valley of Fires Recreation Area

HIKING: Pine Lodge Trail to Chimney Rock and Capitán Peak, West Mountain Trail, Summit Trail, South Base Trail

WINTER ACTIVITIES: Snow accumulations limit access. Any approach would be long and difficult at best.

VEGETATION: Piñon-juniper woodland, ponderosa pine, Douglas fir, Engelmann spruce, aspen

WILDLIFE: Elk, mule deer, turkey, black bear

WATER: Seven Cabins Spring. Water, present but not abundant, is mostly in springs some distance off the ridge crest. You will need to carry your own.

SEASON: Spring through fall

WILDERNESS: The high, rugged east end of the range is protected by the 35,822-acre Capitán Wilderness.

ADMINISTRATION: Lincoln National Forest

THE CAPITÁN MOUNTAINS HAVE THE DISTINCTION OF BEING ONE OF THE NATION'S FEW EAST-WEST TRENDING RANGES, AS WELL AS THE BACKDROP FOR THE LINCOLN COUNTY WAR, ONE OF BILLY THE KID'S HAUNTS, AND THE ORIGINAL HOME OF THE ICON SMOKEY BEAR.

Historical records show that the mountains were called the "Sierra Capitána" as early as 1780. The Capitáns also have interesting prehistory, with Jornada Mogollon sites dating from 900-1200 AD.

The Capitáns are characterized by steep, rocky slopes with numerous adjoining canyons and a ridge capped by several high summits. They are composed of very old rock, from which the overlying sediments have been whittled away by

This view from Capitán Peak (10,083') west towards Palko Peak (10,201'), the range's highest summit, reveals a landscape charred by fire.

erosion. Glaciers helped shape their steep north and south flanks. The range is made up of two sections divided by Capitán Gap at 7,452 feet.

These mountains suffered a disastrous fire that severely charred many of their slopes in 1950. A bear club found clinging to life during that fire was nursed back to health and went on to achieve fame as Smokey Bear, a symbol for forest fire prevention. Even today the Capitáns are a landscape in transition, with many charred trees from recent fires and new growth emerging.

Located in the Lincoln National Forest and designated a national wilderness, the Capitán Mountains have an extensive system of maintained, but rigorous, trails. They are a popular place to hunt deer, bear, and turkey.

LOCATION: Northwest of Ruidoso, between Capitán and the Mescalero Apache Reservation

ACCESS: US 54, 380, 70; NM 532, 37, 48; Forest Roads 107 and 108 on the east side, 579 on the west side.

ELEVATION: 5,700' - 11,973'

GREATEST RELIEF: Sierra Blanca Peak, 4,904'

MAJOR PEAKS: Sierra Blanca Peak (11,973'), Lookout Peak (11,580'), Buck Mountain (10,769'), Nogal Peak (9,957'), Monjeau Peak (9,641')

MAJOR ATTRACTIONS: Three Rivers Petroglyph Site, Ski Apache Ski Resort, Fort Stanton, Ruidoso Downs, Hubbard Museum of the American West

HIKING: Sierra Blanca Crest Trail, Argentina Canyon, Bonito Creek, South Fork Trail, Three Rivers Trail

WINTER ACTIVITIES: Downhill and cross-country skiing, snowshoeing at Ski Apache, which allows access to the upper portions of the mountain. Various roads, most notably Bonito Creek, provide access on the east side. West side approaches would be long and arduous, better suited to hiking below the regional snow line.

VEGETATION: Piñon-juniper woodland, ponderosa pine, Douglas fir, Engelmann spruce, aspen

WILDLIFE: Elk, mule deer, black bear, badger, bobcat, porcupine, turkey

WATER: South Fork, Bonito Creek, Argentina Canyon and numerous springs along the crest make this a well-watered region. The major west side drainage is Three Rivers Canyon.

SEASON: Lower regions of the range are usually open year-round. The upper mountain usually opens up in early June. Snow can fall at any time of the year, and the high country is usually snowbound by early November.

WILDERNESS: The heart of the range is protected by the 48,143-acre White Mountain Wilderness. The status of southern areas on the Apache Reservation is not known.

ADMINISTRATION: Lincoln National Forest

Opposite: *Framed by a forest in transition to fall color, the great summit of Sierra Blanca (11,973') is tinged pink by morning light.*

Sierra Blanca (11,973') from the crest trail in the White Mountain Wilderness.

TOWERING SIERRA BLANCA, IN THE WHITE
MOUNTAIN WILDERNESS, DOMINATES THE
SACRAMENTO MOUNTAINS AND ALL OF
SOUTHEASTERN NEW MEXICO.

This huge extrusive volcanic mountain towers 7,800 feet
above the Tularosa Basin, exhibiting the greatest vertical relief
in New Mexico. It is the easternmost mountain in the
Basin and Range physiographic province, and the southernmost mountain in the US with an elevation that reaches into
the arctic/alpine life zone. It is also the southernmost location
glaciated during the last ice age, and the southernmost
mountain with dominantly Rocky Mountain flora and fauna.

Sierra Blanca, also called White Mountain, is named for the
fact that its summit frequently has snow when surrounding
peaks do not. It has also been known as Old Baldy for its
treeless top. Because of its great height, Sierra Blanca attracts
copious rainfall and, on its east side, supports lush forested
conifers up to its crest. The west side is steep, rugged and
dry with rocky outcrops.

Sierra Blanca is not a young volcano like Mount Taylor
or the Valles Caldera. It emerged between twenty-six and
thirty-eight million years ago, about the same time as the
volcanos in the Gila and Mogollón Ranges were erupting.
The mountain was originally much larger than it is today,
twenty miles in diameter and made up of about 185 cubic
miles of volcanic material. Most of what remains is rock
that cooled slowly within the bowels of the volcano. It is a
testament to its original great size, and to later block faulting
during the formation of the Río Grande Rift, that Sierra
Blanca remains such a significant mountain.

There is evidence of Paleoindian and Archaic people in the
Sierra Blancas, and Jornada Mogollon sites are throughout the mountains. At the Three Rivers Petroglyph Site in
the foothills, more than twenty thousand glyphs created
between 900 and 1400 AD decorate the long basalt ridge
rising from the Tularosa Basin.

Thirty Feet

Anyone who has seen Sierra Blanca Peak in southern New Mexico—whether they were living or playing in Ruidoso, skiing the mountain, hiking its trails, driving along its base in the Tularosa Valley or driving any of the roads to the high country—knows it is a special mountain. Sierra Blanca is the tallest mountain in altitude in southern New Mexico and has the greatest relief of any mountain in the state, rising almost eight thousand feet from its footings in the Tularosa Valley. It also has the distinction of being the southernmost mountain in the United States that shows signs of past glaciation. It is a sacred mountain to the Mescalero band of Apache. And until recently, Sierra Blanca was the southernmost mountain in the United States with an elevation of more than twelve thousand feet.

That last fact is worth noting. Twelve-thousand feet has always held special meaning for me. In the latitudes of the Southern Rockies and the Sierra Nevada Mountains of California, peaks with an altitude over twelve thousand feet usually rise above timberline, and that, in my opinion, puts them in a special class. Sierra Blanca is no exception. With its summit cone rising high above its mantle of forest, Sierra Blanca totally dominates its surroundings. This is a peak inviting exploration. When I climbed Sierra Blanca—twice, in fact—in the early 1970s, its altitude was officially 12,003 feet. It was not a particularly difficult ascent (more of a steep hike, really) but it was definitely a memorable climb. Sierra Blanca is a big peak with a big view, and it always gives me a sense of accomplishment to stand on the summit of a tall mountain. I slept on its summit and felt on top of the world. No other mountains stand near or higher, so it felt almost like being in an airplane.

When new measurements were taken recently, however, Sierra Blanca's altitude was officially lowered by thirty feet, to 11,973 feet, relegating it to that vast fraternity of mountains without distinction—the ones that don't qualify for the 12K club. To those who look at peaks only from afar or with passing indifference, thirty feet might not seem very important. But when you have stood on a summit of a peak that belongs to the 12K club and are a seeker of heights, that thirty feet really does matter.

Despite what the US Geological Survey may say, my feelings for Sierra Blanca haven't changed. I will keep my thirty feet. To me, Sierra Blanca will always be part of that special company of peaks over twelve thousand feet. It was 12,003 feet when I climbed it and in my heart it still is. Even though New Mexico is a mountainous state, we don't have a lot of peaks belonging to the 12K club. I hope they don't go remeasuring any more of our mountains.

Mike Butterfield

The view north from the Sacramento Rim toward Sierra Blanca Peak.

LOCATION: Primarily east and southeast of Alamogordo. Some sources include everything from the Jicarilla Mountains through the mountains south of Alamogordo in the Sacramento Range.

ACCESS: US 54 and 70 from the north and west, US 82 and 24 from the south and east.

ELEVATION: 4,400' - 9,645'

GREATEST RELIEF: Mule Peak, 3,600'

MAJOR PEAKS: Cathey Peak (9,645'), Alamo Peak (9,260'), Sacramento Peak (9,255'), Mule Peak (8,114')

MAJOR ATTRACTIONS: Oliver Lee Memorial State Park, National Solar Observatory at Sacramento Peak, New Mexico Museum of Space History, Cloudcroft, Lincoln National Forest

HIKING: Dog Canyon Trail, Sacramento Rim Trail, Cloud Climbing Rail Trail, Osha Trail, Alamo Canyon, Mule Canyon

WINTER ACTIVITIES: Cloudcroft and Ski Cloudcroft allow easy access to the high country. Cross-country skiers will find abundant opportunities. Ski Cloudcroft is the southernmost downhill ski area in New Mexico.

VEGETATION: Creosote bush, cacti, desert willow, netleaf hackberry, piñon-juniper woodland, pine (ponderosa, yellow), white fir, Douglas fir, aspen, mountain maple

WILDLIFE: Black bear, elk, mule deer, mountain lion, bobcat, coyote, turkey

WATER: Dog Canyon on the west. Río Peñasco and Silver Springs Creek to the East. Springs in Water Canyon and Willie White Canyon, as well as numerous springs and small creeks scattered throughout the range.

SEASON: Year-round in the lower reaches, May through December in the higher elevations

WILDERNESS: No WSA or declared wilderness areas. Numerous private holdings preclude any large roadless tracts. The high crest of the range averages 9,000' for more than twenty miles, though. With over 18,000 acres of non-inventoried road-less area, the Sacramento Rim offers solitude and numerous camping possibilities in a high-elevation forested environment. Although surface water is very limited, caching water at regular intervals is possible because various forest roads cherry-stem into the Rim Trail area.

ADMINISTRATION: Lincoln National Forest

A dramatically different perspective of the Sacramento Mountains, from the Tularosa Valley floor.

THE SACRAMENTO MOUNTAINS HAVE TWO CONTRASTING FACES. THE WEST SIDE IS DEEP AND RUGGED, WITH HIGH, REMOTE CLIFFS AND RIDGES MADE OF SEDIMENTARY ROCK, PRIMARILY LIMESTONE. THE GENTLER EAST SIDE OF THE SACRAMENTOS GRADUALLY DESCENDS UNTIL THE MOUNTAINS GRADE INTO THE SOUTHEAST PLAINS AND THE PECOS RIVER VALLEY.

The Sacramento Escarpment, which rises abruptly to over four thousand feet above the Tularosa Valley, exposes about 500 million years of geologic history and is one of the more spectacular features in the state. Perennial springs and streams in many of the canyons give life to a great diversity of vegetation, with at least eighteen rare plant species. The Sacramentos rose to prominence during early stages of Río Grande rifting, when the Sierra Blanca volcano intruded into the limestones and the Tularosa Basin dropped thousands of feet.

The history of human habitation in the Sacramento Mountains goes back more than ten thousand years. Artifacts and structures have been found from the Paleo-Indian, Archaic, and Jornada Mogollon eras, and most recently and prominently from Apache inhabitants. Prehistoric people walked the mountain trails hunting animals and gathering plants, and chipped stones into knives, scrapers, drills, and hammers. Archaeologists believe the Apaches were in the area by the fifteenth century and took advantage of the reliable water and lush vegetation in Dog Canyon. The Sacramentos were home, hunting ground, and sacred place to the Apache. The famous "Eyebrow Trail" in Dog Canyon and numerous other

Sacramento Mountain locations were the settings for numerous skirmishes between the Apache people and the US Cavalry in the nineteenth century.

Dog Canyon is now part of Oliver Lee Memorial State Park. In the mid-1880s, a Frenchman named François-Jean Rochas, commonly known as "Frenchy," homesteaded at the canyon mouth, built a rock cabin, raised cattle, and cultivated a variety of fruit orchards. He also worked with a transplanted Texas rancher, Oliver Milton Lee, to channel water from the perennial stream at Dog Canyon. Lee established a ranch south of Dog Canyon in 1893 and was instrumental in founding the city of Alamogordo and Otero County.

The developement of the railroad at the turn of the twentieth century played a major role in Sacramento Mountains history. The village of Cloudcroft, at the crest of the Sacramentos, was developed to bring timber from the mountains down to the Tularosa Valley. The "cloud climbing" railroad transported passengers and brought timber down the six thousand feet to Cloudcroft for fifty years. The railroad was abandoned in 1948, but Cloudcroft is still a popular resort.

LOCATION: Near Piñon and extending southeast for nearly 100 miles into Texas.

ACCESS: US 62, 180; NM 137; Cougar Road (County Road 412), Guadalupe Ridge Road (Forest Road 540), Forest Road 67 (from the northwest), Forest Road 27 (SB Falls)

ELEVATION: 4,329' - 8,749'

GREATEST RELIEF: New Mexico: Camp Wilderness Ridge 1,764' ; Texas: Bush Mountain, 4,500'

MAJOR PEAKS: New Mexico: Camp Wilderness Ridge (7,400'+), Lonesome Ridge (7,000'+)
Texas: Guadalupe Peak (8,749), Hunter Peak (8,368'), El Capitán (8,086')

MAJOR ATTRACTIONS: Guadalupe Mountains National Park, Carlsbad Caverns National Park, Sitting Bull Falls, Living Desert Zoological and Botanical State Park

HIKING: Last Chance Canyon, Sitting Bull Falls, Guadalupe Ridge, Lonesome Ridge, Devil's Den Canyon

WINTER ACTIVITIES: No snow activities

VEGETATION: Creosote bush, snakeweed, four-wing saltbush, cacti, agave, mescal bean, Texas madrone, piñon-juniper woodland, ponderosa pine

WILDLIFE: Mule deer, elk, rabbit, bobcat, fox, black bear, mountain lion, bats

WATER: Sitting Bull Canyon and Falls

SEASON: Year-round

WILDERNESS: Carlsbad Caverns National Park and Declared Wilderness (33,125 acres), Guadalupe Mountains National Park (Texas)

ADMINISTRATION: Lincoln National Forest, National Park Service.

Opposite: *Rocky Arroyo in the Seven Rivers Hills area of the Guadalupe Mountains. Not far east of here, the Guadalupe Mountains finally grade into the Pecos River Valley.*

THE GUADALUPE MOUNTAINS, WHICH EXTEND FROM THE VICINITY OF PIÑON, NEW MEXICO, NEARLY ONE HUNDRED MILES SOUTHEAST INTO TEXAS, ARE ONE OF THE FINEST EXAMPLES OF AN ANCIENT MARINE FOSSIL REEF ON EARTH.

About 250 million years ago, a vast tropical ocean covered portions of Texas and New Mexico. When the ancient sea evaporated, the 400-mile-long, horseshoe-shaped Capitán Reef subsided and was buried by a thick blanket of sediments and mineral salts. After the fossil reef had been entombed for millions of years a mountain-building episode and subsequent erosion exposed part of it, creating the Guadalupe Mountains.

This is a landscape of dramatic, thousand-foot, cactus-covered escarpments rising out of the desert terrain, rugged limestone mountains, and deep, curvaceous canyons with sheer walls. The Guadalupe Mountains contain world-class caves. Some of the most unusual and diverse vegetation and wildlife in the Southwest can be found here, including many threatened, endangered, and highly localized species. The Guadalupe Mountains have attracted human habitation for many thousands of years, as evidenced by the presence of Paleoindian artifacts. Pueblo and Mogollon remains, such as large agave roasting ovens and the ruins of strutures, have also been found throughout these mountains. Apaches, including the great chief Gerónimo, occupied the formidable canyons. In the 1860s there were a number of well-known skirmishes between the Mescalero Apache and the cavalry in such places as Last Chance and Dark Canyons. After the coming of the Anglo settlers, outlaws used the limestone caves near the Butterfield Trail to ambush stagecoaches. Captain Pat Garrett, a Texas Ranger at the time, was summoned to discourage this antisocial behavior.

Just southwest of the Guadalupes is a small spur mountain range called the Brokeoff Mountains. They rise to an elevation of only 5,900 feet and are used mainly for grazing sheep.

Opposite: *Looking north at the ancient reef that is now the Guadalupe Mountains.*

LOCATION: Northeast of El Paso and west of Guadalupe Mountains National Park

ACCESS: Unnamed unpaved roads. The closest named roads are US 62, 180; NM 506

ELEVATION: 4,700' – 7,280'

GREATEST RELIEF: Wind Mountain, 2,720'

MAJOR PEAKS: New Mexico: Wind Mountain (7,280') Texas: San Antonio Mountain (7,023')

MAJOR ATTRACTIONS: Guadalupe Mountains National Park

HIKING: No designated trails

WINTER ACTIVITIES: No snow

VEGETATION: Piñon-juniper woodland, shrub oak, mountain mahogany, desert willow, cacti

WILDLIFE: Mule deer, mountain lion, bobcat, coyote, ringtail

WATER: No surface water

SEASON: Year-round

WILDERNESS: BLM Otero Mesa Habitat Area, 500,000-acre roadless area

ADMINISTRATION: Bureau of Land Management. Some state land interspersed.

THE CORNUDAS (HORNED) MOUNTAINS, A SMALL RANGE ALONG THE NEW MEXICO-TEXAS LINE, EMERGE DRAMATICALLY FROM OTERO MESA AND CAN BE SEEN FROM MANY MILES AWAY.

The high point of these mountains is Wind Mountain, an impressive cone-shaped form that rises more than two thousand feet above the surrounding desert floor to an elevation of 7,280 feet. These little-known mountains, well off the beaten track, are interesting for their evidence of early habitation and their unique plants and wildlife.

Numerous petroglyphs and pictographs can be found in the area. The Cornudas were occupied during the prehistoric period and Jornada Mogollon and Puebloan occupants utilized the canyons extensively. Apache groups also inhabited this region throughout the histroric period.

The Cornudas provide habitat for quite a number of unique, rare, and endemic plant species, including the Glass Mountain coral-root, the Turk's head barrel cactus, and a rare orchid. The rugged mountain country also contains unique habitat for raptors such as the peregrine falcon, amphibians and reptiles, several bat species, and desert bighorn sheep. The Cornudas Mountain land snail is a creature found only in this small range.

The high point of the Cornudas Mountains is Wind Mountain (7,280'). The Cornudas, which straddle the Texas-New Mexico border, are a collection of conical and truncated summits.

Along the middle fork of the Gila River, deep within the vast Gila Wilderness, the volcanic character of the Mogollón Mountains is apparent.

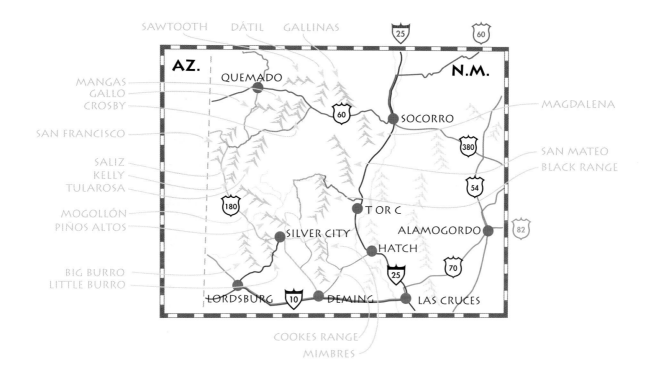

THE DOMINANT LANDFORM IN SOUTHWESTERN NEW MEXICO IS THE DÁTIL-MOGOLLÓN VOLCANIC PLATEAU, WHICH IS APPROXIMATELY ONE HUNDRED MILES IN DIAMETER AND CREATES A TRANSITION ZONE FROM THE COLORADO PLATEAU TO THE BASIN AND RANGE FORMATIONS.

It was formed between twenty-five and forty million years ago during a period of violent, earth-shaking volcanic activity—perhaps some of the greatest events in New Mexico's storied volcanic history. The many large and small mountain ranges in the southwest region are composed of lava flows, tuff, ash, and pumice.

This region contains a large array of wilderness areas, including the state's largest and oldest, the Gila Wilderness, and its third

The Black Range, one of the longest mountain ranges in New Mexico, is also one of the least known. Many trails are disappearing from lack of use. Once called "the wildest wilderness in the West," the heart of the range is protected by the vast Aldo Leopold Wilderness, New Mexico's third largest. This is the view looking south along the crest of the range toward Hillsboro Peak (10,011').

largest, the lesser-known Aldo Leopold Wilderness. With its abundant mountain wilderness and its many rivers, streams, and drainages, this region has tremendous ecological diversity. The Gila country was the last home of the grizzly bear in New Mexico, the setting where Mexican wolves were returned to the wild, and the environs for the endangered Gila cutthroat trout.

The extensive, well-developed trail network in the mountains and forests in the Southwest region includes a substantial segment of the Continental Divide Trail. Its high places are both inviting and accessible to explore. In the Gila Wilderness, seekers of solitude can get as far away from roads as anywhere in New Mexico and star watchers can enjoy one of the darkest places in the continental US.

LOCATION: Northwest of Magdalena

ACCESS: US 60; NM 169; Forest Road 24 in the Bear Mountains, Forest Road 10; County Road E1 in the Gallinas Mountains

ELEVATION: Bear Mountains, 6,500' - 8,221'; Gallinas Mountains, 7,200' - 8,719'

GREATEST RELIEF: Unnamed point in the Bear Mountains, 2,080'

MAJOR PEAKS: Bear Mountains: Sanders (8,221'), Hells Mesa (7,812') Gallinas Mountains: Indian Mesa (8,719'), Gallinas (8,713'), Gallinas Peak (8,442')

MAJOR ATTRACTIONS: Very Large Array (VLA) National Radio Astronomy Observatory

HIKING: No designated trails

WINTER ACTIVITIES: Limited winter activities

VEGETATION: Piñon-juniper woodland, ponderosa pine, gambel oak, grasses

WILDLIFE: Pronghorn, mule deer, elk, javelina, gray fox, Merriam's turkey, Abert's squirrel

WATER: No surface water

SEASON: Spring through fall

WILDERNESS: No declared wilderness or wilderness study areas. Bear Mountains roadless (43,993 acres not inventoried). Gallinas Mountains roadless (43,993 acres not inventoried).

ADMINISTRATION: Cíbola National Forest

THE BEAR AND GALLINAS MOUNTAINS ARE VOLCANIC FAULT-BLOCK MOUNTAINS DOMINATED BY HIGH TABLELANDS AND BROAD BASINS.

They are at the northeast end of the Dátil-Mogollón volcanic plateau, just to the west of the Río Grande rift. The basin area between the Bear and Gallinas ranges contains alluvium from an ancient lake. Elk and pronghorn are plentiful in both ranges, and it is thought that Mexican wolves and grizzly bears lived in the vicinity in the early 1900s.

LOCATION: Northwest of Dátil

ACCESS: US 60; NM 12; Forest Service Roads 59, 14, 6, 6a, 63; Crosby Road

ELEVATION: 7,380' - 9,556'

GREATEST RELIEF: Crosby Mountain, 2,000'

MAJOR PEAKS: Madre Mountain (9,556'), Crosby Mountain (9,483'), Davenport Peak (9,355'), Sugarloaf Mountain (9,155'), Monument Rock (8,541')

MAJOR ATTRACTIONS: Very Large Array(VLA) National Radio Astronomy Observatory

HIKING: Dátil Well Trail, off-trail hikes in Dátil and Crosby Mountains and the rugged peaks of the Sawtooths, Enchanted Tower rock climbing area. The Continental Divide Trail touches the extreme west end of the Sawtooths.

WINTER ACTIVITIES: No paved or plowed roads. Access is difficult.

VEGETATION: Piñon, one-seed juniper, ponderosa, Douglas fir, alligator juniper, gambel oak

WILDLIFE: Porcupine, mule deer, elk, black bear, mountain lion, bobcat, coyote, skunk, porcupine

WATER: Little surface water; Dátil Well Campground

SEASON: April through November, lower reaches year-round

WILDERNESS: No declared wilderness. Sawtooth Mountains roadless (13, 913 acres, not inventoried), Crosby Mountains roadless (22,560 acres, not inventoried), Madre Mountain roadless (72,947 acres, not inventoried)

ADMINISTRATION: Cíbola National Forest

Opposite: *Monument Rock (8,541') in the Sawtooth Mountains greets a new day.*

THE DÁTIL, SAWTOOTH, AND CROSBY MOUNTAINS ARE AT THE NORTHERN END OF THE DÁTIL-MOGOLLÓN PLATEAU IN THE CÍBOLA NATIONAL FOREST, JUST NORTHWEST OF THE TOWN OF DÁTIL.

These mountains are composed of purplish and reddish-gray volcanic tuff, conglomerates, and sandstone. The highest point in all three ragged ranges is Madre Mountain, in the Datils, at 9,556 feet. Nearby Davenport Peak has a fire lookout that can be reached by a steep twelve-mile road from US 60. Thompson Canyon in the Datils has the Enchanted Tower rock climbing area, which is the premier sport climbing area in New Mexico.

Dátil, the Spanish word for date, is thought to refer to either the seed pods of the broad-leafed yucca or the fruit of the prickly pear cactus, which must have looked like dates to early settlers. The name Sierra del Dátil appears on the 1779 Domínguez-Escalante Expedition Map.

The Dátil Well National Recreation Site in the foothills commemorates a major water stop on the "Hoof Highway" or "Beefsteak Trail," along which thousands of cattle and sheep were driven from Springerville, Arizona, to the Magdalena stockyards from the 1880s through the 1950s. Camp Dátil was established by the US Army in 1884 to protect settlers from the Apache.

The Sawtooth Mountains, a western extension of the Dátil Mountains, are aptly named for their sharp-edged appearance. The ridge-like Crosby Mountains, south of the Dátil and Sawtooth ranges, are accessible by trail from a Forest Service Road off NM 12, south of Dátil. The Continental Divide Trail runs through the Sawtooth Mountains. Pie Town, on the edge of the Sawtooths, was established in 1927 and was named for its famous pies, popular with road travellers and local ranchers and cowboys. The pie-making enterprise was more successful than the various attempts at mining. Pie Town is still active today.

Opposite: *Striking from certain vantage points, the Sawtooth Mountains live up to their name. This unnamed summit rises to an elevation of 9,086'.*

LOCATION: South of Quemado

ACCESS: US 60; NM 12, 32, 103; Forest Roads 93, 13, 214

ELEVATION: Gallo Mountains: 7,300' - 9,869'; Mangas Mountains: 7,300' - 10,224'

GREATEST RELIEF: Mangas Mountains: Horse Mountain, 2,600'

MAJOR PEAKS: Gallo Mountains: Escondido Mountain (9,869'), Fox Mountain (9,383'), Gallo Peak (9,225'), Apache Mountain (8,868'); Mangas Mountains: Alegres Mountain (10,244'), Mangas Mountain (9,691'), Horse Peak (9,490')

MAJOR ATTRACTIONS: Nothing in the immediate vicinity

HIKING: The Continental Divide Trail passes through the Mangas Mountains.

WINTER ACTIVITIES: Limited winter sports

VEGETATION: Piñon-juniper woodland, alligator juniper, ponderosa pine, Douglas fir, aspen, cottonwood

WILDLIFE: Mule deer, elk, black bear, coyote, turkey, Mexican spotted owl

WATER: Quemado Lake and Largo Creek

SEASON: Spring through fall

WILDERNESS: Horse Mountain Wilderness Study Area (5,032 acres plus 3,240 additional roadless), Mangas Mountain roadless (12,032 acres not inventoried), Escondido Mountain roadless (37,977 not inventoried)

ADMINISTRATION: Gila National Forest, although physically in Apache National Forest

---

THE GALLO AND MANGAS MOUNTAINS ARE SMALL, ADJACENT RANGES AT THE NORTHWESTERN EDGE OF THE DÁTIL-MOGOLLÓN VOLCANIC PLATEAU.

In a state where the north-south Río Grande Rift is the dominant landform, the east-west alignment of the Gallo and Mangas Mountains is unusual. It testifies to the magnitude of the forces that created this volcanic plateau.

Both ranges lie in the Apache National Forest but are managed by the Gila National Forest. The Continental Divide runs through the Mangas Mountains.

Alegres Mountain (10,244'), New Mexico's own Kilimanjaro, is the high point in the Mangas Mountains.

LOCATION: South of Magdalena

ACCESS: US 60; Forest Service Roads 101, 235

ELEVATION: 6,000'- 10,783'

GREATEST RELIEF: South Baldy, 3,490'

MAJOR PEAKS: South Baldy (10,783'), Timber Peak (10,510'), North Baldy (9,858')

MAJOR ATTRACTIONS: Very Large Array (VLA) National Radio Astronomy Observatory

HIKING: Fifteen designated trails, including the Magdalena Crest Trail to North Baldy, Copper Canyon Trail, South Baldy Loop, Timber Peak Trail

WINTER ACTIVITIES: Lack of paved or plowed roads makes access difficult.

VEGETATION: Piñon-juniper woodland, ponderosa pine, spruce, fir, Apache plume, mountain mahogany, alligator juniper

WILDLIFE: Pronghorn, mule deer, black bear, mountain lion, bobcat, coyote, red and gray fox, bald and golden eagles, Merriam's turkey

WATER: Sawmill Canyon usually has dependable water. Water Canyon is seasonal and might not run throughout the year. Water is more or less continuously available in Copper Canyon. No water on the crest, but hikers with topographic maps should be able to find springs off the crest.

SEASON: Mid-May through November, lower reaches year-round

WILDERNESS: Devil's Backbone Wilderness Study Area, Devil's Reach Wilderness Study Area; 58,656 acre roadless area (not inventoried)

ADMINISTRATION: Cíbola National Forest

Left: *Timber Peak (10,510') in the Magdalena Mountains. These underrated mountains are exceptionally beautiful and deserve more recognition.*

THE LANDSCAPE OF THE MAGDALENA MOUNTAINS CONSISTS OF ROLLING VOLCANIC HILLS, ISOLATED MESAS, DEEP CANYONS, AND FOOTHILLS DOTTED WITH PIÑON, JUNIPER, AND OAK.

These mountains are part of the Basin and Range physiography that characterizes the Río Grand Rift zone, where uplifted mountain ranges alternate with long expanses of flat, dry, down-dropped crustal blocks. The high, sometimes treeless crest of the Magdalenas represents the uplifted halves of east-tilted blocks. These blocks are superimposed on massive calderas, the remains of volcanoes that collapsed about thirty million years ago. Over millions of years, as the crust of the earth expanded, the blocks tilted upward, causing portions to break off and tilt at even sharper angles. The granite core of the mountains is overlaid with limestone.

On the west side of the range is a nearly bare volcanic mountain with a profile that looks like a woman's face. The Spaniards named it Magdalena Peak, for Mary Magdalene. The name was extended to the entire range and, in 1884, to the town of Magdalena.

Ore deposits were first found on the west side of the Magdalenas in 1866. Over the next several decades the area became an important mining district, yielding millions of dollars worth of gold, silver, zinc, and lead. The area around the Magdalena Mountains boomed with small towns and mining activities from 1890 to the 1950s. Only the town of Magdalena still exists.

The Magdalena Mountains are a true sky island, where the substantial variation in elevations—from forty-six hundred to over ten thousand feet—provides for a wide diversity of vegetation. Because the flat Plains of San Agustín are just to the west, storms tend to hit the mountains with an intensity that replenishes the various mountain ecosystems. With the variety of habitats and the availability of water, wildlife is abundant and varied. This is one of the premier birding areas in the state, with red-faced and olive warblers, zone-tailed hawks, Montezuma quail and an amazing variety of owl species. The high mountains, deep canyons, and open rolling hills offer exceptional recreational opportunities.

The view from the crest of the Magdalena Mountains, looking north toward an unnamed peak (10,281'), the bare summit of North Baldy (9,858'), and the Sierra Ladrones on the distant skyline.

LOCATION: Between Socorro and Truth or Consequences, west of the Río Grande

ACCESS: US 60; NM 1, 52, 107; Forest Service Roads 549, 52, 330, 478, 140, 225, 76

ELEVATION: 6,000' - 10,336'

GREATEST RELIEF: San Mateo Mountain, 3,750'

MAJOR PEAKS: Blue Mountain (10,336'), Vicks Peak (10,252'), San Mateo Mountain (10,145'), San Mateo Peak (10,139'), Mount Withington (10,115'), Apache Kid Peak (10,048')

MAJOR ATTRACTIONS: Elephant Butte Lake State Park

HIKING: Grassy Lookout to Mulligan Peak, Blue Mountain Trail, Vicks Peak Trail, Apache Kid Trail, Indian Creek Trail, Water Canyon and Coffee Pot Canyon Trails, Potato Canyon Trail, Pink Glissade Waterfall Trail, Mount Withington

WINTER ACTIVITIES: No paved or plowed roads. Access is difficult.

VEGETATION: Grasses, piñon, three species of juniper, yucca, saltbush, mountain mahogany, Apache plume, spruce, fir

WILDLIFE: Pronghorn, mule deer, black bear, mountain lion, bobcat, coyote, wild turkey

WATER: Water Canyon, Coffee Pot Canyon, Potato Canyon (seasonal), Coffee Pot Spring, San Mateo Spring. Numerous springs throughout the region might run seasonally. Check with the Forest Service.

SEASON: Mid-April through November; lower reaches year-round

WILDERNESS: Apache Kid Wilderness (44,650 acres plus 86,000 acres additional roadless), Withington Wilderness (18,869 acres)

ADMINISTRATION: Cíbola National Forest

Opposite: *The rugged country of Cooney Canyon and Potato Canyon in the Withington Wilderness, seen from atop Mount Withington (10,115') in the little visited San Mateo Mountains. A-L Peak (9,648') rises on the left.*

THE LARGE, WILD, NORTH-SOUTH SAN MATEO A RANGE CONTAINS AT LEAST SEVEN PEAKS OVER TEN THOUSAND FEET.

They also have two designated wilderness areas, the Withington Wilderness in the north and the Apache Kid Wilderness in the south.

These mountains are a north-south trending uplifted fault block within the Dátil-Mogollón volcanic field. The uplifted volcanic rocks that compose them were formed in major eruptions that occurred between twenty-eight and twenty-four million years ago, during a period of intense volcanic activity in the western part of this continent. The most spectacular ash flow tuff deposits are at Vicks Peak. Thousand-foot cliffs form the southernmost escarpment of the range. Erosion and weathering over the last twenty million years have carved numerous deep canyons, including the spectacular Peñasco and Point of Rocks Canyons.

These mountains were a favored hunting ground, sanctuary, and stronghold for the Apache. A remote, rugged, starkly beautiful wilderness area and mountain are named after the famous renegade, the Apache Kid. The Kid was a White Mountain Apache born near Globe, Arizona, in the 1860s. He was a friend of the US Army and a scout in the Gerónimo campaigns before he fell out of favor and become an outlaw. His four-year campaign of terror in the San Mateo Mountains ended in 1894 when he was shot and killed in an ambush. He was buried next to ten-thousand-foot Apache Kid Peak in the heart of the wilderness that came to bear his name. Another famous native son, the great Apache leader Victorio, also haunted the San Mateos. Vicks Peak is named after him.

After the conflicts with the Apache abated, prospectors came more frequently to mine the local gold, silver, and copper. Rosedale Canyon, around Vicks Peak, and the Goldsboro district on the south side of the mountains supported successful ventures for a while.

Opposite: *Looking east up West Red Canyon in the San Mateo Mountains, near the Apache Kid Wilderness boundary. These mountains receive few visitors, although they are less than three hours from Albuquerque.*

LOCATION: Southeast of Reserve

ACCESS: NM 12, 435; Forest Roads 233, 94

ELEVATION: 6,500' - 9,802'

GREATEST RELIEF: Milligan Mountain, 2,316'

MAJOR PEAKS: Eagle Peak (9,802'), Buzzard Peak (9,692'), Wagontongue Mountain (8,892'), John Kerr Peak (8,868'), Milligan Mountain (8,409')

MAJOR ATTRACTIONS: Nothing in the immediate vicinity

HIKING: Continental Divide National Recreation Trail

WINTER ACTIVITIES: Lack of paved roads makes access difficult. Forest Roads 233 and 94 might allow access to cross-country skiing and snowshoeing when there is sufficient snow cover. It is advisable to check road status with the Forest Service. Access might be muddy.

VEGETATION: Piñon-juniper woodland, alligator juniper, ponderosa pine, Douglas fir, aspen, cottonwood

WILDLIFE: Mule deer, elk, black bear, mountain lion

WATER: Negrito Creek on the south side, Tularosa River on the west side, Squirrel Springs Canyon on the north side

SEASON: Spring through fall

WILDERNESS: Eagle Peak roadless (92,870 acres not inventoried), John Kerr Peak roadless (31,584 acres not inventoried), Long Canyon roadless (31,208 acres not inventoried)

ADMINISTRATION: Gila National Forest

Left: *The lower reaches of the Tularosa Mountains near Reserve, with the Tularosa River snaking its way along the valley bottom.*

LOCATION: Between Luna and Reserve

ACCESS: US 180; Forest Roads 232, 209

ELEVATION: 6,500' - 8,980'

GREATEST RELIEF: Whiterocks Mountain, 2,980'

MAJOR PEAKS: Aspen Mountain (8,980'), Whiterocks Mountain (8,827'), Dillon Mountain (8,740'), Monument Mountain (8,401'), Black Bull Peak (8,361')

MAJOR ATTRACTIONS: Nothing in the immediate vicinity

HIKING: San Francisco River Box Trail, WS Mountain Trail, Dangerous Park Trail, Cottonwood Trail, Aspen Mountain Trail

WINTER ACTIVITIES: US 180 crosses range. Cross-country skiing and snowshoeing may be possible at the north and south forest roads at the highway's crest when there is adequate snow.

VEGETATION: Piñon-juniper woodland, oak, ponderosa pine, aspen

WILDLIFE: Mule deer, elk, black bear, mountain lion

WATER: San Francisco River and its tributaries, Trout Creek, and Centerfire Creek are the principal waterways in the region. Blue River, which drains the west side, is mostly in Arizona.

SEASON: Spring through fall

WILDERNESS: Blue Range Wilderness (29,304 acres), Largo Canyon Creek roadless (12,032 acres not inventoried)

ADMINISTRATION: Gila National Forest, although the range is physically in Apache National Forest

---

THE SAN FRANCISCO MOUNTAINS ARE ON THE FAR WESTERN BORDER OF NEW MEXICO, SOUTH OF LUNA, IN THE APACHE NATIONAL FOREST.

This well-vegetated range with deep canyons is bordered by the San Francisco River to the east and north and the Blue River to the west. The San Francisco Mountains spill into the Blue Range Wilderness, which is a relatively small, moist, primitive wilderness with few developed trails. The wilderness is a potential Mexican wolf reintroduction area. A portion of the Mogollón Rim escarpment lies in the San Francisco Mountains, in the southwestern part of the wilderness.

Whiterocks Mountain (8,827'), though not the highest summit in the San Francisco Mountains, dominates the south end of that range.

LOCATION: Southwest of Reserve

ACCESS: US 180; NM 12, 435

ELEVATION: Kelly Mountains, 5,200' - 7,962'
Saliz Mountains, 5,600' - 7,587'

GREATEST RELIEF: Kelly, 2,405'

MAJOR PEAKS: Kelly Mountains: Apache Peak (7,962'), Kelly Mountain
(7,667'); Saliz Mountains: unnamed (7,587')

MAJOR ATTRACTIONS: None nearby

HIKING: Saliz Pass Trail, Frying Pan Canyon Trail

WINTER ACTIVITIES: NM 435 is paved for 16 miles and is the main
access to the higher terrain in the Mogollón Mountains, although the
approach is long and mostly on dirt roads. Cross-country skiing and show-
shoeing possible when there is sufficient snow cover.

VEGETATION: Piñon-juniper, ponderosa pine, oak, willow

WILDLIFE: Pronghorn, mule deer, black bear, mountain lion,
bobcat, coyote

WATER: Saliz Canyon on the west side of the Saliz Mountains; the San
Francisco River between the Saliz and the west side of the Kelly Mountains.
The ridge crests of both ranges are basically dry, with seasonal water.

SEASON: Spring through fall

WILDERNESS: No declared wilderness or wilderness study areas

ADMINISTRATION: Gila National Forest

Right: *The wooded summits of the Kelly Mountains hint at what lies to the southeast, in the
higher and better-watered Mogollón Mountains.*

Topping out at just under 11,000', Whitewater Baldy is the highest peak in the Mogollón Mountains. It anchors the vast, surprisingly lush and well-watered high country at the west end of the Gila Wilderness.

LOCATION: South of Reserve

ACCESS: US 180; NM 78, 159, 435, 15

ELEVATION: 4,600' - 10,895'

GREATEST RELIEF: Sacaton Mountain, 4,358'

MAJOR PEAKS: Whitewater Baldy (10,895'), Willow Mountain (10,783'), Mogollón Baldy (10,770'), Sacaton Mountain (10,658'), Black Mountain (10,643'), Center Baldy (10,535'), Grouse Mountain (10,135'), Bearwallow Mountain (9,920'), Turkeyfeather Mountain (9,771')

MAJOR ATTRACTIONS: Gila Cliff Dwellings National Monument, Gila Hot Springs, Catwalk

HIKING: Mogollón Crest Trail, Whitewater Baldy Trail, Catwalk Trail, Grouse Mountain Trail, Gila River Middle Fork and West Fork Trails

WINTER ACTIVITIES: NM 435 is paved for 16 miles and is the main access to the higher terrain in the Mogollón Mountains, although the approach is long and mostly on dirt roads. Cross-country skiing and snowshoeing with sufficient snow cover.

VEGETATION: Douglas fir, Engelmann spruce, aspen, oak, piñon-juniper woodland

WILDLIFE: Mule deer, white-tailed deer, elk, black bear, mountain lion, fox, coyote, badger, porcupine

WATER: Gila River (West fork, Middle Fork, East Fork), Whitewater Creek (North Fork and South Fork), and San Francisco River are the major waterways. Numerous creeks and streams drain and feed the principal waterways in the vast Mogollón complex. Springs along the crest, which usually run year-round except in very dry years include Bead, Hummingbird, Hobo, Apache, and Black Mountain. Check with the Forest Service regarding the status of springs before a backpack trip.

SEASON: Lower reaches year-round, though summer may prove too hot. The higher regions usually are free of snow by mid-May but sometimes drifts remain as late as early June. The high country is usually closed by mid-November, but in dry years the season may extend into early December.

WILDERNESS: Gila Wilderness (558,065 acres plus 166,500 acres additional roadless), Devils Creek roadless area (100,000 acres inventoried)

ADMINISTRATION: Gila National Forest

THE MOGOLLÓN MOUNTAINS ARE AN EXTENSIVE, PRECIPITOUS RANGE LOCATED ON THE SOUTH-WEST SIDE OF THE DÁTIL-MOGOLLÓN VOLCANIC PLATEAU IN THE GILA NATIONAL FOREST.

The Mógollons, like the nearby San Francisco, Tularosa, Kelly, Saliz, and Piños Altos ranges, were formed during a period of great volcanic activity in southern New Mexico between twenty-five and forty million years ago. They all consist of lava flows, tuffs, welded ash flows, pumice, and other volcanic materials. During the same period of volcanism, two huge calderas formed after the expulsion of tremendous quantities of lava. Portions of caldera rim are still visible in the Mogollóns. A series of earthquakes also changed the landscape through extensive faulting. All this activity helped produce areas of great vertical relief and north-south trending mountain ranges such as the Mogollóns.

The region's numerous hot and warm springs are reminders of the fiery volcanic events that produced the mountains. These healing waters apparently attracted early Native Americans to the Mogollón Mountain area, just as they attract legions of hikers and outdoor enthusiasts today. There are few remains from the earliest inhabitants, but archaeologists have uncovered an abundance of artifacts and remains from the Mimbres culture, dating from 300 BC to 1300 AD. The early Mimbres people domesticated plants such as maize, beans, and squash, and constructed semi-permanent dwellings in the ground called pithouses. Around 1000 AD, they began to replace their plain brown-and-red pottery with pots decorated with intricate black-and-white designs and built masonry structures, some high up in the mountain cliffs. Remains of these dwellings are found all through the Gila Wilderness, but the best examples are at the Gila Cliff Dwellings National Monument in the Mogollón Mountains. Like many Puebloan groups of the period, the Mimbres abandoned their village sites and left the area.

It was primarily the Chiricahua and Mimbres bands of the Apache who later settled and hunted in the Mogollón-Gila country. The famous chief, Gerónimo, is said to have been born near the Gila River headwaters around 1829. The Apaches were formidable defenders of their territory. They ruled the area through much of the nineteenth century, until Gerónimo's surrender in 1886.

Things changed quickly, however, in the 1890s, when silver and gold were discovered in the hills. A great mining boom over the next twenty years put the town of Mogollón on the map. In 1915, Mogollón was New Mexico's leading mining district, with the most productive mine being the Little Fannie. The road to the mines was steep and harrowing, so the ores were transported largely by horse-drawn wagons. Primitive as this was, the mines were incredibly productive. In 1913, approximately $1.5 million worth of gold and silver was extracted from the Mogollón mines, which was about forty percent of New Mexico's precious metals total that year. The town of Mogollón suffered numerous fires and floods through the years, but managed to survive them. Today, Mogollón is one of the state's premier ghost towns and still has some year-round residents.

The North Fork of Whitewater Creek, known as a quality trout stream, tumbles down from the high country of the Mogollón Crest and descends west until it disappears underground at the mouth of Whitewater Canyon near the town of Glenwood.

Above: *The view from the summit of Bearwallow Mountain (9,920') the view takes in a vast area of seemingly untracked wilderness with virtually no sign of human presence.*

Right: *Bigtooth Maples color a side canyon along the road to the ghost town of Mogollón and the high country beyond.*

BLACK RANGE & MIMBRES
MOUNTAINS

LOCATION: Between the Plains of San Agustín and Faywood

ACCESS: NM 52, 59, 152, 35, 163; Forest Road 150

ELEVATION: 5,000' - 10,165'

GREATEST RELIEF: McKnight Mountain, 3,405'

MAJOR PEAKS: Black Range: McKnight Mountain (10,165'), Hillsboro Peak (10,011'), Reeds Peak (10,011'), Diamond Peak (9,850'), Lookout Mountain (8,872'); Mimbres Mountains: Sawyer's Peak (9,668'), Seven Brothers Mountain (8,690'), Thompson Cone (7,971')

MAJOR ATTRACTIONS: Caballo Lake State Park, Gila Cliff Dwellings National Monument

HIKING: Black Range/Continental Divide Trail, Emory Pass/Hillsboro Peak Trail, Sawyer's Peak Trail, Mimbres River Trail

WINTER ACTIVITIES: Emory Pass is kept open and allows access to higher terrain for cross-country skiing and snowshoeing when there is adequate snow.

VEGETATION: Piñon-juniper, ponderosa pine, spruce, fir, aspen, grasses

WILDLIFE: Mule deer, black bear, mountain lion, fox, coyote

WATER: Mimbres River, Black Canyon, Diamond Creek, McKnight Canyon, Iron Creek on the west side. Las Animas, Percha Creek, Circle Seven Canyon on the east side, Mimbres Lake, as well as numerous springs, on or near the ridge crest (check with Forest Service for status)

SEASON: Lower elevations are open year-round. On the upper slopes, the south side is open by mid-April and the north side by mid- to late May, until snows close access in mid- to late November.

WILDERNESS: Aldo Leopold Wilderness (202,016 acres plus 198,000 additional roadless acres), Sawyer's Peak roadless (121,000 acres inventoried)

ADMINISTRATION: Gila National Forest

Left: *The diffused light from the smoke of distant forest fires makes for an exceptional sunrise in this view from Emory Pass in the Black Range.*

THE NARROW, NORTH-SOUTH BLACK RANGE, ONE OF THE STATE'S LONGEST RANGES, STRETCHES BETWEEN SAN AGUSTÍN PLAINS AND FAYWOOD FOR NEARLY A HUNDRED MILES.

Also known as Sierra de Los Mimbres and Sierra Diablo (devil mountain), the Black Range is rough, untamed country that is known for its steep slopes, narrow canyons, and difficult access. It runs through the Aldo Leopold Wilderness Area and the Gila National Forest and contains a substantial segment of the Continental Divide National Recreation Trail. The Mimbres Mountains, at the southern end of the Black Range, are considered a continuation of that range.

Like many uplifted blocks adjacent to the Río Grande Rift, the Black Range has a central core of Precambrian granite overlaid by ocean-bottom sediments and covered by thick layers of volcanic rock. Numerous ruins in the Mimbres Valley indicate that the earliest settlers in the region were the Mimbres. Spanish settlers living along the Río Grande were fearful of these remote, dark mountains. They called them the devil mountains, because of the deep, treacherous canyons and the fierce, well-armed Apaches, led by the likes of Mangas Coloradas, Cochise, Nana, Victorio, and Gerónimo.

Gerónimo passed through the range with some frequency on his way to one of his hideouts near Chloride. Lieutenant W.H. Emory, guided by Kit Carson, crossed the Black Range with the Army of the West in 1846, through the pass that now bears his name.

Gold and silver were discovered in the Hillsboro, Lake Valley, Chloride, and Kingston areas in the late 1870s. The mining boom, with new settlements sprouting on the east side of the range, lasted for more than a decade. One of the more remarkable discoveries was the "Bridal Chamber" near Lake Valley, an underground room containing enormous quantities of pure silver that was easily mined and loaded directly onto railroad cars.

The Aldo Leopold Wilderness was named for the conservationist who was the driving force behind the creation of the world's first formally protected wilderness area, the Gila. The Aldo Leopold Wilderness, separated from the Gila Wilderness in 1932, is now the third-largest wilderness area in the state.

Opposite: *Often thought of as a single crest, the Black Range is anything but that. This view near McKnight Mountain (10,165') looks south towards Hillsboro Peak (10,011') and takes in the Las Animas Canyon complex on the range's east side in the Aldo Leopold Wilderness.*

LOCATION: Northeast of Silver City

ACCESS: NM 35, 15, 152

ELEVATION: 7,000' - 9,029'

GREATEST RELIEF: Signal Peak, 2,200'

MAJOR PEAKS: Black Peak (9,029'), Signal Peak (9,001'), Scott Peak (8,347')

MAJOR ATTRACTIONS: Silver City, Piños Altos (town)

HIKING: Signal Peak Trail, Tadpole Ridge Trail

WINTER ACTIVITIES: Cross-country skiing and snowshoeing are possible when there is sufficient snow.

VEGETATION: Aspen, Engelmann spruce, Douglas fir, ponderosa pine

WILDLIFE: Elk, mule deer, black bear, mountain lion, fox, bobcat

WATER: No water along crest of the range. Cherry Creek drains south and Trout Creek drains north from a low pass that splits the range. Sapello Creek enters the Gila River along the north side of the range.

SEASON: Spring through fall

WILDERNESS: Northwestern end of the range is protected by the Gila Wilderness.

ADMINISTRATION: Gila National Forest

THE PIÑOS ALTOS (TALL PINES) MOUNTAINS, JUST NORTH OF SILVER CITY, ARE A SMALL, NORTH-WEST-SOUTHEAST TRENDING RANGE COMPOSED PRIMARILY OF MIOCENE VOLCANIC ROCKS.

Placer gold was first discovered here by a party of California prospectors in 1860. As was frequently the case in this part of the state, the Apaches made life difficult for miners and settlers in what they considered their territory. Fort Bayard was established in 1866 as a frontier cavalry post at the foot of the Piños Altos range to keep the Apaches at bay. It was not until two years after the Civil War, in 1867, that placer lode mining was resumed, reaching a peak in 1868. Gold, silver, copper, lead, and zinc were profitably mined in the area through the 1920s.

LOCATION: South of the Black Range and north of Deming

ACCESS: US 180; NM 26; Cookes Canyon Road, Dipping Springs Road, Greenleaf Mine Road

ELEVATION: 5,200' - 8,404'

GREATEST RELIEF: Cookes Peak, 3,108'

MAJOR PEAKS: Cookes Peak (8,404'), Massacre Peak (5,687')

MAJOR ATTRACTIONS: City of Rocks State Park, Rockhound State Park

HIKING: Cookes Peak is primarily a rock scramble.

WINTER ACTIVITIES: No winter activities

VEGETATION: Desert shrubs, piñon-juniper, ponderosa pine, Arizona cypress, fir, oak

WILDLIFE: Mule deer, gray fox, coyote, bobcat, golden eagle, prairie falcon, Gila whiptail

WATER: Riley Spring, which is difficult to locate and may not be reliable.

SEASON: Spring and fall are the best seasons. The range can be hiked year-round, but summer can be extremely hot.

WILDERNESS: Cookes Range Wilderness Study Area (19,608 acres plus 4,240 additional roadless acres)

ADMINISTRATION: Bureau of Land Management, state lands

THE COOKES RANGE IS A SMALL CLUSTER OF MOUNTAINS NORTH OF DEMING WITH ONE PROMINENT SUMMIT, COOKES PEAK.

The peak is a regional landmark that can be seen from many miles away in all directions, and its granite, craggy summit has reminded some of the Matterhorn. The range and peak were named after Captain Philip St. George Cooke, a leader of the Mormon Battalion in Kearny's army, which passed through here in 1846-47. Prior to Captain Cooke, in the late 1700s, the peak was called Cerro de Los Remedios, hill of remedies. Several of the ridges that form the backbone of the Cookes Range rise between one thousand and three thousand feet above the surrounding desert plains. These ridges are broken up by numerous deep canyons and secondary ridges that direct any rainfall and moisture into the closed drainage basin of the Mimbres River. This is wild, rugged country.

The Cookes Range is another example of a sky island, with an impressive diversity of habitat ranging from coniferous woodland to desert grassland and desert shrub. Among the interesting, unusual plants and animals here are the night-blooming cereus, a stand of Arizona cypress (far to the east of that tree's normal range), goshawks, several endemic species of terrestrial snails, and the Sonoran Mountain kingsnake. It is also considered a potential location for the reintroduction of desert bighorn sheep.

There are major petroglyph and pueblo sites in the range. For centuries, the range was part of the Apache territory and used as a lookout because of its high vantage point. The Butterfield Stage line was routed around the mountain because of the presence of reliable springs, most notably Cookes Springs.

The Cooke mining camp was established when lead-silver ore was found here in 1876. The ore was hauled down the wagon road and netted several million dollars. The small town of Cookes Peak, created in 1889, was in operation until 1914. It was a tough place where killings were common occurrences.

The US Army established Fort Cummings to protect travelers and the mines from Apache attacks. The mountain southeast of Cookes Peak is called Massacre Peak because a wagon train from Juárez was ambushed there by Victorio's band in 1879. The victims of the massacre were buried at the base of the mountain.

Opposite: *A landmark for miles around, Cookes Peak (8,404') commands a wide view and was used as a lookout by the Apache Indians. The Butterfield Stage was routed around the mountain to take advantage of the reliable springs.*

LOCATION: Between Lordsburg and Silver City

ACCESS: US 180; NM 90; Forest Roads 851 (Redrock Road), 136 (Tyrone Road)

ELEVATION: 5,000' - 8,035'

GREATEST RELIEF: Burro Peak, 2,055'

MAJOR PEAKS: Burro Peak (8,035'), Jacks Peak (7,986'), Ferguson Mountain (7,966'), Bullard Peak (7,064'), Schoolhouse Mountain (6,370')

MAJOR ATTRACTIONS: Silver City, Shakespeare (ghost town)

HIKING: Continental Divide Trail passes through southern portion of mountains.

WINTER ACTIVITIES: No winter activities

VEGETATION: Piñon-juniper, chaparral, desert shrubs, grassland, mesquite

WILDLIFE: Mule deer, gray fox, coyote, mountain lion, black bear, endangered Chiricahua leopard frog

WATER: Very little surface water. The Gila River defines the northern boundary of range.

SEASON: Year-round, except after heavy rain or snowfall (muddy)

WILDERNESS: Gila Middle Box inventory unit (19,660 acres plus 21,985 additional roadless acres), Big Burro Mountains State roadless (22,182 acres), national forest roadless (45,497 acres not inventoried)

ADMINISTRATION: Gila National Forest

THE BIG AND LITTLE BURRO MOUNTAINS ARE PARALLEL RANGES SOUTHEAST OF SILVER CITY, SEPARATED BY THE MANGAS VALLEY.

The Little Burro Mountains are only eight miles long and located primarily on private property, so they are generally not accessible to the public. The Big Burro Mountains are a twenty-mile long wooded range at the southernmost extension of the Gila National Forest. The mountains are composed of Precambrian granite, volcanic rocks, and conglomerates washed from adjoining ranges by drainage from the upper Gila River Basin. The Continental Divide Trail passes over Burro Peak and across a shoulder of Jacks Peak.

Looking from City of Rocks State Park west to the Burro Mountains.

Prehistoric people mined turquoise from these mountains; their stone axes and red pottery have been found west of St. Louis Canyon. The Pueblo people had been mining for the blue-green gem for centuries before the Spanish arrived, prizing it for religious, ornamental, and trade purposes. Turquoise from the Burro Mountains and the Cerrillos Hills has been found at archeological sites more than a hundred miles away.

The largest single vein of turquoise ever discovered, the Elizabeth Pocket in the well-named Azure Mine, was opened in 1893 and produced $2 million worth of stones. Tiffany's in New York featured turquoise from this mine for many years. Other minerals that have been tapped from the Big Burros include copper, gold, silver, manganese, and fluorite. Tyrone and Leopold, now ghost towns, were established by the Phelps Dodge Corporation to work nearby cop-

per deposits. Phelps Dodge spent more than $1 million in 1917 to make Tyrone a model mining town, with Spanish mission architecture and a large tree-lined plaza. Tyrone thrived until 1921, but little now remains of either town.

The Big Burro Mountains contain numerous old mine and forest roads, some of which provide access to summits. At one time there was a Smithsonian Institution solar radiation laboratory on South Peak.

167

Of Bears & Devils

I like bears. I like everything about them. Their presence indicates I am in wild country, where man is only an interloper. (Okay, I have bears in my neighborhood when drought forces them from the mountains in search of food. But, heck, the Sandía Mountains are wild country—just not large enough, or a complete enough ecosystem, to contain foraging bears. Albuquerque has severely truncated their range, so I am really living in the bears' backyard.)

I like bears, I just don't like camping with them. This may sound odd coming from someone who has spent over thirty-five years backpacking, often solo, in the mountains where old bruin lives. But what I don't know makes me feel better. This was brought home to me one time in the Black Range, the Diablo Mountains of southern New Mexico. I had decided to backpack up the Mimbres River Canyon, then on up to the top of the range for some photography. As I approached the trailhead, a black bear ran across the road. This fellow was not large, perhaps 150 pounds, and not really black, but cinnamon colored with a charcoal-gray head. I had never seen a bear up close before, so it was pretty exciting.

Thinking I'd try for a photo, I retrieved my gear from the jeep and walked to a point where I thought the bear might head up the canyon. Only then did it occur to me that although the bear wasn't that big, it was still a bear, and I was standing in its path with only a camera. Prudence dictated a tactical retreat to my vehicle.

I alerted a family camping nearby, but they didn't seem worried. I thought of all of the trips I had taken into the back country without ever seeing a bear. Perhaps old man bear had passed close by when I was unaware. Or perhaps centuries of hunting have given *Ursus Americanus* a healthy fear of upright bipeds and he steers way clear.

The place where I was going to set up camp, not many miles away near the trail's first dependable water source, was in the bottom of a canyon—the same narrow canyon, I now realized, in which my bear was wandering. I knew the bear was probably heading as far away from humans as possible, fast as he could. That didn't keep me from being obsessed with the fact that a bear was in the neighborhood, though. I didn't abandon my hike, but I did start many miles away and much higher up, at Emory Pass. If there were bears higher up it was okay, as long as we didn't come face to face.

Mr. Bear can own the mountain. So long as we don't meet, I can camp in peace.

Mike Butterfield

Black Range vista from Emory Pass.

The distinctive triple summits known as the Tres Hermanas (three sisters) are a regional landmark despite their modest elevation.

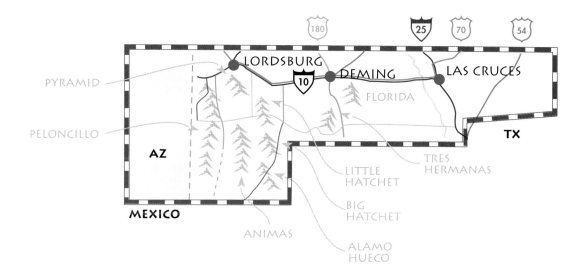

PYRAMID

PELONCILLO

AZ

MEXICO

180

LORDSBURG

10

DEMING

FLORIDA

LITTLE
HATCHET

BIG
HATCHET

ANIMAS

ALAMO
HUECO

TRES
HERMANAS

25   70   54

LAS CRUCES

TX

IN THE FAR SOUTHWESTERN CORNER OF NEW MEXICO ARE SOME OF THE STATE'S MOST REMOTE, INACCESSIBLE, HOT, ECOLOGICALLY FASCINATING MOUNTAINS.

The Bootheel, named for the way it juts south from this otherwise boxy state, generally includes the lands south of I-10 and west of the Río Grande rift. New Mexico has a Bootheel only because of the Gadsden Purchase of 1854, when the United States bought what is now southern Arizona and southwestern New Mexico from Mexico. This substantial chunk of real estate was acquired for $10 million, about $340 a square mile, as part of the proposed southern route for the transcontinental railroad. Few visitors venture into this remote part of the state, but with its muted mountain beauty, its exotic wildlife and plants, and its colorful history, it warrants a look.

The Bootheel is part of the Basin and Range Province, where small, geographically isolated mountain ranges are separated by wide, arid basins. This separation between the mountains creates sky islands, so that the various mountain ranges contain unique ecological niches. The entire region straddles the

A fast-moving snow squall at sunrise approaches cone-shaped North Pyramid Peak (6,008') in the proposed Pyramid Mountains Wilderness.

Chihuahuan and Sonoran Deserts and shares their wildlife and plant species. It is also influenced by the uplands and riparian areas of the Gila country to the north and the wild, warmer Sierra Madre to the south. As a result, the Bootheel is a crossroads for a wide assortment of creatures and plants and contains more rare and endangered species than any other part of the state. The Gray Ranch in the Animas Mountains, where the Animas Foundation and other groups have been working to promote and protect the region's biodiversity, is one of the nation's most significant ecological research sites. While the Bootheel may not contain the highest, most spectacular or most inviting mountains in the state, it offers ample wonders and wilderness rewards to the adventurous.

LOCATION: South of Lordsburg

ACCESS: I-10; NM 338; County Road A9, C92, Animas Road

ELEVATION: 4,268' - 6,008'

GREATEST RELIEF: North Pyramid Peak, 1,550'

MAJOR PEAKS: North Pyramid Peak (6,008'), South Pyramid Peak (5,910')

MAJOR ATTRACTIONS: Shakespeare (ghost town)

HIKING: No other designated trails. The Continental Divide Trail passes through the southern portion.

WINTER ACTIVITIES: No snow activities

VEGETATION: Desert shrubs, yucca, grasslands, juniper

WILDLIFE: Javelina, deer, mountain lion, coyote, hawks

WATER: No surface water

SEASON: Year-round, although spring and fall are best. Summer is hot.

WILDERNESS: Pyramid Mountains Complex proposed wilderness (35,709 acres plus 10,064 additional roadless acres on adjacent state land)

ADMINISTRATION: Bureau of Land Management; some state and private land intermixed

THE STEEP PYRAMID MOUNTAINS ARE CHARACTERIZED BY DEEP CANYONS, ROLLING HILLS, AND GENTLY SLOPING ALLUVIAL FANS DESCENDING FROM THE RIDGES AND PEAKS.

Reflecting the geologic history of the area, the Pyramids are a north-south fault block approximately twenty-two miles long with the remains of a volcanic caldera forming much of the southern end. They get their name from Pyramid Peak, the conical volcanic neck at the north end of the range.

Pyramid Peak, rising fifteen hundred feet above the desert floor, was a welcome landmark for travelers in the nineteenth century because it had a fresh water spring. It was used extensively by the Butterfield Stage Company on the long, hot run between Mesilla and Tucson.

The Pyramid Mountains have been mined for copper, gold, silver, lead, zinc, and uranium. Shakespeare, at the center of the former mining district, is one of New Mexico's best-preserved ghost towns. Briefly home to some three thousand silver miners during the early 1870s, it was largely abandoned after a few booms by 1890. In the 1930s, a family converted the town into a private ranch, and some of the old mining-era buildings were restored and preserved. The small mining town of Pyramid, just to the south, was established in the early 1800s and very short-lived. The Pyramid Range was the site of a mining hoax; an unscrupulous entrepreneur planted Brazilian and African diamonds in some of the mines to entice potential investors.

The New Mexico Wilderness Alliance has inventoried the Pyramid Mountains and identified more than 45,000 acres potentially suitable for wilderness designation. The only intrusions in this wild area have been a few livestock developments. These little-known mountains provide excellent opportunities for solitude (easy to find in the Bootheel), and for geological sightseeing and horseback riding.

At sunset, shadow and light play across the face of Rimrock Mountain (5,785') on the north end of the Pyramid Mountains in the proposed Pyramid Mountains Wilderness.

LOCATION: West of Lordsburg and Animas

ACCESS: NM 9, 80; County Roads C27, C35, C47, A12

ELEVATION: 4,500' - 6,570'

GREATEST RELIEF: Bunk Robinson Peak, 1,665'

MAJOR PEAKS: Mount Baldy Peak (6,570'), Black Mountain (6,545'), Black Point (6,467'), Guadalupe Mountain (6,450'), Bunk Robinson Peak (6,241')

MAJOR ATTRACTIONS: Granite Gap Mining Town

HIKING: Few designated trails or water sources, but some good hiking and exploring

WINTER ACTIVITIES: No snow activities

VEGETATION: Desert grassland, piñon-juniper, oak woodlands, Fremont cottonwood, Arizona sycamore, netleaf hackberry, great diversity of cactus species

WILDLIFE: Desert bighorn sheep, javelina, mule deer, Coue's white-tailed deer, mountain lion, coatimundi, black bear, a great diversity of amphibians, reptiles, and birds

WATER: Blackwater Hole

SEASON: Year-round

WILDERNESS: Peloncillo Mountains Complex proposed wilderness (194,513 acres)

ADMINISTRATION: Coronado National Forest

THE PELONCILLO MOUNTAINS, STRETCHING ALONG THE ARIZONA-NEW MEXICO BORDER, ARE A LONG, NARROW RANGE WITH IMPRESSIVE ROCK FORMATIONS, CANYONS, CLIFFS, AND SHARPLY RISING VOLCANIC PEAKS.

Geologically, the Peloncillos are a linear upthrust block of granites and subsequent sedimentary rocks invaded by a variety of more recent volcanic formations, including tuffs and lava flows. Erosion has created aprons of wide-sloping plains called bajadas. Peloncillo, little baldy in Spanish, accurately describes the range's barren summits, especially in contrast to the higher and greener Chiricahua Mountains to the west. The southern portion of the range lies in the Coronado National Forest.

The Peloncillo Mountains sit close to the New Mexico-Arizona border within the proposed Peloncillo Mountains Wilderness.

The Peloncillos encompass the northern reach of the Sierra Madre Occidental from Mexico and straddle the Sonoran and Chihuahuan Deserts. The merging of all these different ecosystems results in a stunning variety of plant and animal life. The wide diversity of plant communities includes desert grasslands and shrubs, piñon-juniper woodlands, oak woodlands, juniper savannah, riparian vegetation, and Mexican species of oaks and piñon pine. Many of the plant species found here exist nowhere else in New Mexico. The mountains support an especially diverse cactus population. Notable among the many unique species of amphibians, reptiles, and birds are the Gila monster, the Arizona coral snake, and the elegant trogon (a gorgeous bird). The Peloncillos also contain habitat for the jaguar and the Mexican wolf.

These mountains were a stronghold for the Chiricahua Apaches, and this is where Gerónimo surrendered. A major route to mining camps including Tombstone, Clanton Draw and Skeleton Canyon ran along the Pelencillos. The first stagecoach passed by Steins Peak in 1857, connecting San Antonio with San Diego. The following year, the historic Butterfield Stage was launched along the same route. Steins, now a ghost town, was born in 1880, when the Southern Pacific Railroad arrived. Chinese workers blasted many tons of rock in the area to make rail beds for the railroad. The nearby Granite Gap Mine was also active for several decades. Granite Gap was mined for silver, lead, zinc, and copper into the 1920s. Legends of buried gold bars, stagecoach robberies, and smugglers are part of the Peloncillos lore.

Opposite: *Desert bloom anchors this view westward across the top of the Peloncillo Mountains and proposed Penocillo Mountains Wilderness toward the higher, greener Chiracahua Mountains just over the border in Arizona. Photo by Peter Greene.*

LOCATION: Southeast of Deming

ACCESS: NM 11, 141, 143, 198, 497

ELEVATION: 4,200' - 7,295'

GREATEST RELIEF: Florida Peak, 3,000'

MAJOR PEAKS: Florida Peak (7,295), Gym Peak (7,106'), South Peak (7,084'), Baldy Peak (6,920')

MAJOR ATTRACTIONS: Rockhound and Pancho Villa State Parks

HIKING: Rockhound State Park hiking trails

WINTER ACTIVITIES: No snow activities

VEGETATION: Creosote, mesquite, hackberry, juniper, scrub oak, cacti

WILDLIFE: Desert bighorn sheep, pronghorn, coyote, prairie dog, badger, mountain lion, Persian ibex

WATER: No surface water

SEASON: Year-round, although spring and fall best. Summer can be brutally hot.

WILDERNESS: Florida Mountain Wilderness Study Area (22,336 acres)

ADMINISTRATION: BLM, some state land and private parcels

Left: *Boldly vertical Castle Rock in the Florida Mountains stands in stark contrast to the soft muted colors of sunrise.*

Collectively, the two ranges are an uplifted block of older rocks punctuated by calderas and other volcanic deposits. They are separated by Florida Gap. The north side of the Florida Mountains has low ridges and brushy hogbacks, while the south side has steep declines and jagged ridges.

The Florida (flower) Mountains were named by sixteenth-century Spanish explorers, who were most likely enraptured by the spectacular poppy blossoms carpeting the slopes during a wet spring. They were referred to on a 1762 map as the Sierra Floridas. It has been said that from a distance these volcanic mountains resemble a battleship—an analogy reminiscent of those other lonely sentinels, Ship Rock and Cabezón. It is ironic that ships have so often been envisioned in the deserts of New Mexico, so far from the sea.

A few small caves in the Florida Mountains show evidence of prehistoric occupation. During the nineteenth century they were well known as part of Apache territory, valued for their reliable springs, plant life, and protective cover. The Apaches and the US Army skirmished frequently here and throughout southern New Mexico. In 1877, Lieutenant Henry Wright from nearby Fort Cummings led a contingent of Ninth Cavalry Buffalo Soldiers and Navajo Scouts in search of a Chiricahua Apache campsite in the Florida Mountains. They found the camp but retreated because they were greatly outnumbered. The famed Apache chief Victorio was wounded in these mountains, by prospectors, near Bear Springs.

In the late 1800s, low grade lead-zinc ores, gold, and silver were discovered and mined in the Florida Mountains. The Mahoney and Silver Cave mines were the largest producers.

Rockhound State Park in the Little Florida Mountains has been an attraction since it opened in 1966 for its abundance of colorful rock specimens: geodes, agates, thunder eggs, jasper, onyx, quartz, and obsidian (known as Apache tears). There are several trails in the park that wind through these volcanic mountains to accommodate geologic and mineral exploration and observation.

The Florida Mountains display their serrate crest. Their distinctive profile, visible from miles away, reminds many of a battleship. Florida Peak (7,295')
is the highest point.

LOCATION: South of Deming and slightly northwest of Columbus

ACCESS: NM 11; County Roads C15 (Waterloo Turnoff), C9

ELEVATION: 4,200' - 5,802'

GREATEST RELIEF: North Sister, 1,602'

MAJOR PEAKS: North Sister (5,802'), Middle Sister (5,786'), South Sister (5,614')

MAJOR ATTRACTIONS: Pancho Villa State Park

HIKING: No designated trails

WINTER ACTIVITIES: No snow activities

VEGETATION: Desert grassland, shrubs, and cacti; mesquite, creosote, chaparral, sage

WILDLIFE: Mule deer, pronghorn, badger, javelina, rabbit, coyote, eagles, hawks

WATER: No surface water

SEASON: Year-round, although spring and fall are best. Summer is hot.

WILDERNESS: No declared wilderness, wilderness study areas, or roadless areas

ADMINISTRATION: Bureau of Land Management, some state and private land intermixed

THE TRES HERMANAS MOUNTAINS (THREE SISTERS) ARE A LOW BUT DISTINCTIVE RANGE JUST NORTHWEST OF COLUMBUS.

The row of three prominent peaks is a landmark for travelers approaching the US-Mexico border. These mountains are very old, with 35-million-year-old quartz at the core and a thick covering of more recent sedimentary and volcanic rocks.

Gold, silver, lead, and zinc were discovered in these mountains around 1887. A cave on the eastern slope has an outstanding display of fluorescent minerals.

The ghost town of Hermanas is a few miles to the east of the mountains. Hermanas was principally a railroad town on the El Paso and Southwestern Railroad line. Established in the early 1900s, it became a base for local mining, farming, and livestock ventures. The population probably never exceeded 150 people, and the post office shut down in 1925.

Opposite: *A classic upper Sonoran Desert scene plays out over a timeless landscape: The Tres Hermanas (three sisters) Mountains in the soft colors of day's end make a postcard-perfect view.*

THE BIG HATCHET, LITTLE HATCHET, AND ALAMO HUECO MOUNTAINS ARE PART OF THE BASIN AND RANGE PROVINCE THAT EXTENDS INTO SOUTHWESTERN NEW MEXICO, SOUTHEASTERN ARIZONA, AND NORTHERN SONORA, MEXICO.

These are rugged desert ranges that feature highly eroded volcanic mountains, rolling limestone hills, and gently sloping alluvial fans. The Big Hatchet Mountains consist of faulted and tilted Paleozoic limestone and Cretaceous shale and sandstones. Big Hatchet Peak is one of the more spectacular mountains in New Mexico, with its limestone cliffs towering more than four thousand feet above the desert floor.

These mountains, like other Bootheel ranges, are located at the ecological crossroads of the temperate mountains to the north and the tropical Sierra Madre Occidental to the south, as well as two major deserts, the Chihuahuan and the Sonoran. The result is an enormous diversity of plants and animals. Notables include Chihuahuan pine, walnut, seepwillow, evergreen oak, and three varieties of pincushion cacti. Caves in the area provide habitat for a large number of bats, and the steep cliffs provide nesting areas for many kinds of raptors. Other wildlife species of note include desert bighorn sheep, javelina, coatimundi, various bunting, the giant spotted whiptail, and an endemic snail. This area also provides potential habitat for jaguar, thick-billed parrots from Mexico, and Aplomado falcons.

The caves of the Alamo Hueco Mountains contain an abundance of prehistoric cultural resources, some of which are nationally significant. Archaeologists have found prehistoric tools in the Little Hatchet Mountains that are evidence of early turquoise mining. In the late1800s, turquoise, gold and copper again lured prospectors to the Little Hatchets.

Opposite: *Rising a full 4,000' over the surrounding desert playa, the Big Hatchet Mountains in the proposed Big Hatchet Wilderness host a seasonal display of desert bloom. To those not familiar with New Mexico's Bootheel, a scene like this is a pleasant surprise.*

LOCATION: South of Hachita

ACCESS: I-10; NM 146, 9, 81

ELEVATION: Big Hatchets: 4,270' - 8,441'

Little Hatchets: 4,800' - 6,639'

Alamo Huecos: 4,800' - 6,810'

GREATEST RELIEF: Big Hatchet Peak (4,071')

MAJOR PEAKS: Big Hatchets:

Big Hatchet Peak (8,441')

Little Hatchets: Hachita Peak (6,585')

Alamo Huecos: Pierce Peak (6,159'),

Hat Top Mountain (5,168')

MAJOR ATTRACTIONS: Pancho Villa State Park

HIKING: No designated trails

WINTER ACTIVITIES: No snow activities

VEGETATION: Evergreen oak, piñon, Chihuahuan pine, desert scrub and grassland, hackberry

WILDLIFE: Desert bighorn sheep, javelina, mule deer, pronghorn, coatimundi, bats, golden eagles, Montezuma quail, Sonoran Mountain kingsnake

WATER: No surface water

SEASON: Year-round

WILDERNESS: Big Hatchet Wilderness Study Area (48,270 acres) plus 100,000 additional roadless acres. All of Big Hatchet Mountain Range managed as a state game refuge. Alamo Hueco Wilderness Study Area (16,264 acres) plus additional roadless (15,720 acres)

ADMINISTRATION: Bureau of Land Management, NM Department of Game and Fish

THE ANIMAS MOUNTAINS ARE CHARACTERIZED BY STEEP RIDGES THAT RISE DRAMATICALLY FROM THE DESERT FLOOR, JUNIPER-DOTTED ROLLING HILLS, DEEP CANYONS, AND GENTLE SLOPES. They have coniferous forests at the highest elevations and piñon-juniper woodland, desert shrubs and grasses, and riparian areas with cottonwoods below.

These mountains are one of the larger sky islands, with a unique diversity of plants and animals. Among the numerous special-status plant species are the night-blooming cereus and several other rare cacti. As for wildlife, the Animas Mountains, with biotic influence from the Chihuahuan and Sonoran deserts and the Sierra Madre in Mexico, have the greatest concentration of endangered species in New Mexico.

There are approximately 130 species of reptiles, javelina, coatimundi, a lowland leopard, a Sonoran mud turtle, zone-tailed hawks, Mexican wild turkeys, and potential habitat for the federally-endangered Mexican wolf. Jaguar might be present on a transient basis. The 500 square-mile Gray Ranch, one of the largest ranches in New Mexico, provides conservation for the more than 700 species of plants, 75 mammals, 50 reptiles and amphibians, and more than 170 species of breeding birds. The Gray Ranch was origi-nally purchased by the Nature Conservancy then transferred in 1993 to the Animas Foundation, an organization dedicated to protecting the natural values of the ranch while maintaining the cultural and economic heritage of the Bootheel.

LOCATION: South of Animas

ACCESS: I-10; NM 338

ELEVATION: 5,000' - 8,532'

GREATEST RELIEF: Animas Peak, 3,200'

MAJOR PEAKS: Animas Peak (8,532')

MAJOR ATTRACTIONS: Nothing close

HIKING: Continental Divide Trail, few other designated trails

WINTER ACTIVITIES: No snow activities

VEGETATION: Desert shrubs, piñon-juniper, spruce, fir, cottonwood

WILDLIFE: Pronghorn, javelina, coatimundi, bear, moun-tain lion, Mexican wild turkey, Sonoran mud turtle

WATER: Indian Creek, Black Bill Spring. Check at Gray Ranch headquarters on status of springs and creeks.

SEASON: Year-round

WILDERNESS: Animas Mountains roadless (60,010 acres)

ADMINISTRATION: Animas Foundation and Nature Conservancy at Gray Ranch. Permission is required for public access.

The Animas Mountains and surrounding lands, protected as a nature preserve by the Animas Foundation, are directly connected to Mexico's Sierra Madre Mountains. The meeting ground of many bioregions, they are one of the most ecologically diverse regions in the entire United States. The Animas Mountains Area proposed wilderness.

Dem Bones

Well, here I am on another photo shoot, camping out of the back of my Jeep. I am near the Tres Hermanas Mountains, near Deming, but this could be anywhere in the Bootheel and, by extension, the Chihuahuan Desert. The wind is blowing a lonely tune and I have the same feeling I always get in the desert. Everything is scraped bare, nothing is superfluous. It feels ancient. I can feel it in my bones.

The winds, sometimes strong, are usually katabatic winds from the mountains. It is important to have desert mountains. They give the land character and three-dimensionality. They help define the space. The mountains are all around me but, like the desert, seem to have little to distinguish them. I find that strangely comforting. I can see why some people become desert rats. I'm not talking about the metastasizing populations of the desert megacities; I mean the souls who prefer the space and solitude that only the open desert provides. They are always friendly and accommodating, as if my being there makes me a kindred spirit.

All around are ranges and hills, tough to get to and even tougher to get to know. Unlike the people, the landscape doesn't seem to care whether you are here or not. After the people left the towns that sprang up around the big strikes, the harsh desert conditions made quick work of them. Only a few buildings or foundations are left. On a moonless night near a ghost town, in the desert breeze, you can almost hear the clank and rattle of a long abandoned bar.

And always the mountains remain, aloof, indifferent to man's goings-on. Scarred by mining activity, open pits and shafts around their bases, the mountains remain. In the high desert on a clear night, the sky seems to go on forever. Stars by the billions populate the heavens. Out of reach, out of time, it just is. I can lie on my back and stare into the cosmos for hours. And even on a moonless night, the mountains are darker than the sky. Even when I can barely see them, I sense them.

When the moon is out, it can be tough to sleep. I get up and wander about, and I think about the Moody Blues singing: "Cold hearted orb that rules the night, Removes the colours from our sight, Red is gray and yellow white, But we decide which is right. And which is an illusion?"* After a while, I return to my camp and drift into slumber. All around me the mountains remain, ancient, scraped bare, their essence revealed. The bones of the earth, for my pleasure.

Mike Butterfield

* Moody Blues: *The Day Begins* from *Days of Future Passed.*

The Florida Mountains, with their summer heat, rugged nature, and lack of trails, can be a hiking challenge. Spring is perhaps the best time to visit, when vegetation is in full bloom and temperatures are moderate.

South Truchas Peak (13,102') is the highest summit in the Santa Fe Range and crowns the high, rugged crest of the southern Sangre de Cristo Mountains. On the left is East Pecos Baldy (12,529'). To the right is Middle Truchas Peak (estimated 13,060').

The mountain list that follows was compiled for two reasons: to provide a comprehensive resource for peak baggers who are planning adventures, and in an attempt to set a standard in New Mexico as to what a peak really is. My starting point was the list of named peaks in Herbert Ungnade's classic *Guide to the Mountains of New Mexico*, published in 1965. I updated the elevations using *National Geographic* topographic software and expanded the list to include all unnamed summits over 11,000 feet.

For easy reference, the list is sorted both by elevation and by mountain name. The list by elevation includes ranking numbers for summits that I believe qualify as sovereign peaks, as well my criteria: shoulder drop and distance from their nearest neighbor, measured in a straight line from peak to peak.

Other states have criteria for determining whether peaks are sovereign or just the shoulder of a neighboring mountain. In Colorado, for example, the Mountain Club and the US Geological Survey collaborate to set their criteria, especially for 14ers. They look for a minimum shoulder drop of 300 feet and half a mile distance from the nearest neighbor. As the New Mexico Mountain Club confirmed when I called, our state has no such guidelines.

To establish New Mexico criteria, I chose one mountain as a benchmark: Old Mike, the Wheeler Range peak which dominates the view from the Moreno Valley. It is named on all topographic maps, is over 13,000 feet in elevation, has a shoulder drop of 253 feet, and is a mile from its nearest neighbor, Wheeler Peak.

Several other peaks in the Wheeler Range have shoulder drops of at least 200 feet so, to be inclusive, I decided to use 200 feet as a minimum shoulder drop for peaks over 11,000 feet to be considered sovereign in New Mexico. (The shoulder drop of Simpson Peak, also named on the topographic maps, is at most 70 feet. I have walked over this "peak" to climb Old Mike, and, in my opinion, it does not qualify as sovereign.) I was more exclusive with peaks in the 10,000 to 11,000 foot elevations and used a 300 foot shoulder drop as a standard for sovereignty for those peaks. I also determined that New Mexico sovereign peaks should be at least half a mile from the nearest neighbor.

In the elevation list, peaks over 11,000 feet that meet these criteria have a number indicating their rank among sovereign peaks. Peaks that do not qualify are listed but not ranked. (The exception is Middle Truchas Peak. It has a shoulder drop of only 166', but a personality and identity all its own.)

As this list reveals, New Mexico has many mountains over 11,000 feet that deserve more attention, recognition and study.

Mike Butterfield

Rank	Peak or Mountain	Elev. (ft.)	Closest Neighbor	Drop	Dist. (mi.)	Range (or Region)
1	Wheeler Peak	13,161	Old Mike Peak	301	1.10	Taos
	Mt. Walter	13,133	Wheeler Peak	73	0.40	Taos
2	Old Mike	13,113	Wheeler Peak	253	1.25	Taos
3	South Truchas	13,102	Middle Truchas	282	0.50	Truchas
4	West Truchas [1]	13,066	South Truchas	257	0.45	Truchas
5	Middle Truchas [6]	13,060	West Truchas	166	0.45	Truchas
6	North Truchas	13,024	Middle Truchas	644	1.00	Truchas
	Simpson Peak	12,976	Old Mike Peak	76	0.50	Taos
7	Big Costilla Peak [4]	12,931	Vintrero	761	4.00	Culebra
	un 12,885 [6]	12,885	North Truchas	185	0.50	Truchas
8	Vintrero	12,881	un 12,383	776	2.25	Culebra
9	Lake Fork Peak	12,881	Fairchild (un 12,819)	541	1.00	Taos
10	State Line Peak [3]	12,867	un 12,383	855	1.20	Culebra
11	Cerro Chimayosos	12,841	un 12,515	765	1.00	Santa Barbara
12	Jicarita Peak	12,835	un 12,828	307	0.75	Mora
13	un 12,828	12,828	Jicarita Pk	300	0.75	Mora
14	Fairchild (un 12,819)	12,819	un 12,728	549	0.75	Taos
15	Venado Peak	12,734	Latir Peak	354	1.00	Latir
	un 12,728	12,728	Simpson Peak	150	0.50	Taos
16	Gold Hill	12,711	un 12,217	741	1.50	Columbine-Hondo
17	Latir Peak	12,708	Venado Peak	313	1.25	Latir
18	Sheepshead	12,696	un 12,885	476	0.75	Truchas
	Red Dome	12,681	Old Mike Peak	181	1.00	Taos
19	Santa Barbara Peak (un 12,626)	12,650	Little Jicarita Peak	460	1.25	Santa Barbara
20	Vallecito Mountain	12,643	Lake Fork Peak	783	2.00	Taos
21	Trouble	12,622	un 12,828	322	3.00	Mora
22	Santa Fe Baldy	12,622	Capulín Peak	657	2.50	Santa Fe
23	Virsylvia Peak	12,594	Venado Peak	308	1.00	Latir
24	Little Costilla Peak	12,584	un 11,902	854	1.25	Cimarrón
	Little South Truchas [6]	12,560	South Truchas Peak	160	0.50	Truchas
	un 12,550	12,550	Venado Peak	180	0.50	Latir
25	East Pecos Baldy	12,529	Pecos Baldy	319	1.00	Truchas
26	un 12,515	12,515	un 12,382	305	1.00	Truchas
27	un 12,510	12,510	Jicarita Peak	265	1.00	Mora

SOVEREIGN PEAKS (WITH A SHOULDER DROP OF 200 ' OR MORE) ARE RANKED. UN MEANS THE PEAK IS UNNAMED.

Rank	Peak or Mountain	Elev. (ft.)	Closest Neighbor	Drop	Dist. (mi.)	Range (or Region)
28	Pecos Baldy	12,500	East Pecos Baldy	290	1.00	Truchas
	un 12,496	12,496	Fairchild (un 12,819)	146	0.50	Taos
29	Jicarilla Peak	12,494	Sheepshead	274	2.25	Truchas
	un 12,483	12,483	Santa Fe Baldy	183	0.75	Santa Fe
	Kachina Peak (un 12,481)	12,481	Lake Fork Peak	181	0.85	Taos
	un 12,469	12,469	Sheepshead	129	0.40	Truchas
30	un 12,456	12,450	Cabresto Peak	324	0.85	Latir
31	un 12,453	12,453	un 12,885	273	1.25	Truchas
32	un 12,450	12,450	Vintrero	345	1.20	Culebra
33	Lew Wallace Peak	12,449	Old Mike Peak	229	1.25	Taos
34	Cabresto Peak	12,448	un 12,456	312	0.50	Latir
35	Baldy Mountain	12,441	Touch-Me-Not Mountain	1,341	3.80	Cimarrón
36	Lake Peak	12,409	Penitente Peak	309	0.50	Santa Fe
37	un 12,383	12,383	un 12,450	203	1.40	Culebra
	un 12,382	12,382	un 12,515	172	1.00	Santa Barbara
38	Capulín Peak	12,357	Santa Fe Baldy	657	2.50	Santa Fe
39	Pueblo Peak	12,305	un 12,156	593	0.50	Taos
40	Taos Cone	12,277	Red Dome	217	0.90	Taos
41	Little Jicarita Peak	12,266	un 12,515	276	1.65	Santa Barbara
	Penitente Peak	12,249	Lake Peak	189	0.50	Santa Fe
	un 12,225	12,225	un 12,885	165	2.15	Truchas
42	un 12,217	12,217	Gold Hill	237	1.50	Columbine-Hondo
43	un 12,170	12,170	un 12,456	320	0.50	Latir
44	Trampas Peak	12,170	un 12,453	980	3.50	Truchas
45	un, 12170 [6]	12,170	Pueblo Peak	410	0.50	Latir
46	un 12,165	12,165	Latir Pk	225	2.00	Latir
47	Frazer Mountain	12,163	Wheeler Peak	223	2.00	Taos
48	un 12,116	12,116	Baldy Mountain	240	0.75	Latir
49	Lobo Peak	12,115	Flag Mountain	542	3.00	Columbine-Hondo
	un 12,114	12,114	Sheepshead	174	1.00	Truchas
50	un 12,110 (Doctor Peak)	12,110	Penitente Peak	220	1.00	Santa Fe
51	un 12,050 [6]	12,050	un 12,217	310	1.00	Columbine-Hondo
	Tesuque Peak	12,047	Lake Peak	110	1.00	Santa Fe
52	Baldy Mountain	12,046	un 12,116	240	0.75	Latir

Rank	Peak or Mountain	Elev. (ft.)	Closest Neighbor	Drop	Dist. (mi.)	Range (or Region)
53	Touch-Me-Not Mountain	12,045	Baldy Mountain	945	3.80	Cimarrón
54	un 12,025	12,025	Latir Peak	285	2.10	Latir
55	un 12,020 [6]	12,020	East Pecos Baldy	235	0.75	Truchas
56	un 12,014 (Larkspur Peak) [2]	12,014	Lew Wallace Peak	410	1.15	Taos
57	un 12,012	12,012	Kachina Peak (un 12,481)	202	1.00	Taos
58	un 11,997	11,997	Pecos Baldy	377	0.85	Truchas
	Larkspur Peak (12,014) [2]	11,992	un 12,014	154	0.50	Taos
59	un 11,981	11,981	un 12,025	321	0.75	Latir
60	un 11,979	11,979	un 12,020	309	1.50	Truchas
61	South Fork Peak	11,978	Vallecito Mountain	358	1.75	Taos
62	Sierra Blanca Peak	11,973	Lookout Peak	828	1.30	Sierra Blanca
63	Pinabete Peak	11,953	Cabresto Peak	613	2.00	Latir
64	Flag Mountain	11,946	un 11,802	366	1.15	Columbine-Hondo
65	Cerro Vista	11,939	Cerro del Oso	319	6.00	Mora
	Cerro Olla	11,932	Cerro Vista	172	2.25	Mora
	Peñasco Grande	11,931	un 12,136	106	1.50	Las Vegas
66	un 11,921	11,921	Little Costilla Peak	224	1.10	Cimarrón
67	un 11,912	11,912	South Fork Peak	572	1.25	Taos
68	un 11,903	11,903	un 12,114	203	0.50	Truchas
	un 11,893	11,893	Gold Hill	179	1.60	Columbine-Hondo
69	un 11,849	11,849	un 11,792	674	1.00	Columbine-Hondo
70	un 11,821	11,821	Sierra Mosca	481	1.50	Truchas
71	un 11,802	11,802	Lobo Peak	222	1.25	Columbine-Hondo
72	Sierra Mosca	11,801	un 11,821	461	1.50	Truchas
73	un 11,792	11,792	un 12,050	252	0.75	Columbine-Hondo
74	Relica Peak	11,784	Tunnel Hill	524	1.15	Columbine-Hondo
75	Clear Creek Mtn. (Mt. Phillips)	11,730	Comanche Peak	482	1.00	Cimarrón
76	un 11,691	11,691	Cerro Vista	281	1.50	Mora
77	Tunnel Hill	11,668	Gold Hill	208	1.50	Taos
78	Elk Mountain	11,661	Spring Mountain	601	5.00	Las Vegas
79	un 11,656	11,656	un 11,979	406	1.00	Truchas
	Bull of the Woods Mountain	11,645	Frazer Mountain	131	1.15	Taos
80	un 11,610	11,610	Vermejo Peak	382	2.00	Cimarrón
81	Vermejo Peak	11,610	un 11,921	310	3.00	Cimarrón

Rank	Peak or Mountain	Elev. (ft.)	Closest Neighbor	Drop	Dist. (mi.)	Range (or Region)
82	Lookout Peak	11,580	Sierra Blanca Peak	410	1.30	Sierra Blanca
83	un 11,571	11,571	Tesuque Peak	271	2.15	Santa Fe
84	Tschicoma Mountain (Chicoma)	11,561	Polvadera Peak	1,142	3.50	Jémez
85	Tolby Peak	11,527	Clear Creek Mountain	479	1.50	Cimarrón
86	un 11,500 [6]	11,500	Cerro Olla	230	1.00	Mora
87	un 11,455	11,455	Cebolla	360	5.00	Las Vegas
88	un 11,437	11,437	un 12,025	243	1.25	Latir
89	Ash Mountain (south)	11,430	Ash Mountain (north)	707	1.00	Cimarrón
90	un 11,410 [6]	11,410	Capulín Peak	230	1.10	Santa Fe
91	Grouse Mesa	11,403	Brazos Peak	607	2.00	Brazos
92	Cuchillo de Fernando	11,395	un 11,045	615	1.25	Rincón Mountains
93	un 11,387	11,387	Baldy Mountain	224	1.85	Latir
94	un 11,385	11,385	un 12,110	325	1.00	Truchas
95	un 11,375	11,375	un 11,281	275	1.00	Truchas
96	un 11,353	11,353	un 12,284 (Colorado)	333	3.50	Cimarrón
97	The Dome	11,336	South Truchas Peak	486	3.50	Truchas
98	un 11,312	11,312	un 11,437	522	1.50	Latir
99	Black Mountain	11,302	Gold Hill	452	2.50	Columbine-Hondo
100	Mount Taylor	11,301	La Mosca	736	1.10	San Mateo
	Comanche Peak	11,299	Clear Creek Mountain	119	1.00	Cimarrón
101	Brazos Peak	11,288	Grouse Mesa	498	2.00	Brazos
102	un 11,276	11,276	Cerro Vista	300	1.75	Mora
103	un 11,275	11,275	un 11,312	369	1.00	Latir
104	Cerro del Oso	11,255	un 11,500	435	3.00	Mora
105	Redondo Peak	11,254	Cerros del Abrigo	2,554	6.30	Jémez
106	Greenie Peak	11,249	un 11,081	729	4.50	Latir
107	Ash Mountain (North) [6]	11,240	Little Costilla Peak	494	1.50	Cimarrón
108	Polvadera Peak	11,232	Tschicoma Mountain	813	3.50	Jémez
109	Van Diest Peak	11,222	un 11,081	462	3.00	Valle Vidal
	Taos Peak	11,220	Taos Cone	120	2.50	Taos
110	Ortiz Peak	11,209	un 11,081	370	2.00	Valle Vidal
	Spring Mountain	11,180	Elk Mountain	120	5.00	Las Vegas
111	un 11,177	11,177	Ortiz Peak	477	2.50	Latir
112	Green Mountain	11,165	Touch-me-not	560	1.50	Cimarrón

Rank	Peak or Mountain	Elev. (ft.)	Closest Neighbor	Drop	Dist .(mi.)	Range (or Region)
113	un 11,123	11,123	un 11,437	396	1.75	Latir
114	un 11,116	11,116	un 11,987	496	3.50	Truchas
115	Aspen Peak	11,109	un 11,212	250	0.75	Santa Fe
116	un 11,00	11,000	un 10,570	920	3.00	Cimarrón
117	Agua Fria Peak	11,086	Angel Fire Mtn. (Cienequilla Mtn.)	669	2.25	Cimarrón
118	un 11,081	11,081	Ortiz Peak	241	2.00	Valle Vidal
119	un 11,067 [6]	11,067	un 11,061	213	1.50	Brazos
120	un 11,061 [6]	11,061	un 11,067	207	1.50	Brazos
121	un 11,055 (Angel Fire Peak)	11,055	Osha Mountain	801	4.50	Rincón Mountains
122	un 11,045	11,045	Cuchillo de Fernando	265	1.25	Rincón Mountains
123	La Mosca	11,036	Mount Taylor	471	1.10	San Mateo
124	un 11,033 [6]	11,033	Greenie Peak	213	2.00	Valle Vidal
125	Big Red (un 11,024)	11,024	Comanche Peak	445	1.50	Cimarrón
	un 10,980	10,980	un 11,610	480	1.75	Cimarrón
	un 10,970	10,970	un 11,067	360	2.00	Brazos
	Peñascoso Mountain	10,970	un 12,510	242	3.50	Santa Barbara
	Brazos Ridge	10,963				Tusas
	Sawmill Mountain	10,962				Latir
	Jawbone Mountain	10,960				Tusas
	San Antonio Peak	10,935				Tusas
	Garcia Peak	10,925	Clear Creek Mountain			Cimarrón
	Cerro Toledo	10,925				Valles Calderas
	Canjilón Mountain	10,913				Tusas
	Whitewater Baldy	10,895				Mogollón
	Black Mountain	10,895	Bear Mountain	640	1.50	Cimarrón (Philmont)
	Gallina Peak	10,893	Lobo Peak	300	2.30	Columbine-Hondo
	Osha Mountain	10,885	un 11045	369	2.45	Rincón Mountains
	Lucero Peak	10,820	un 11,912	460	1.50	Taos
	Picurís Mountain	10,810				Picurís Range
	Round Mountain	10,809				Pecos
	Tetilla Peak	10,800				Latir
	Willow Mountain	10,783	Whitewater Baldy	683	2.50	Mogollón
	South Baldy	10,783				Magdalena Mountains
	Mogollón Baldy	10,770	Center Baldy	1,120	3.00	Mogollón

Peak or Mountain	Elev. (ft.)	Closest Neighbor	Drop	Dist. (mi.)	Range (or Region)
Buck Mountain	10,769	Lookout Mountain	489	2.00	Sierra Blanca
un 10,761	10,761	Tschicoma Peak	466	1.50	Jémez
Peñasco Amarillo	10,719				Tusas
un 10,705 [6]	10,705	Peñasco Amarillo	548	4.66	Tusas
Sandía Crest	10,678				Sandía Mountains
Bear Mountain	10,665	Black Mountain	410	1.50	Cimarrón (Philmont)
Sacaton Mountain	10,658				Mogollón
Black Mountain	10,643	Center Baldy	423	1.50	Mogollón
un 10,347 (Sierra de Toledo)	10,347	Cerro Toledo	337	1.75	Valles Calderas
The Knob	10,625	un 12,510	459	2.90	Santa Barbara
Cieneguilla Mountain	10,616	Agua Fria Peak	164	2.25	Cimarrón
Santa Fe Dome	10,613				Santa Fe
un 10,612	10,612	un 10,610	302	1.00	Brazos
un 10,610	10,610	un 10,612	300	1.00	Brazos
San Pedro Peak	10,605				Sierra Nacimiento
Elephant Rock	10,556				Latir
Thompson Peak	10,554				Santa Fe
Center Baldy	10,535	Black Mountain	315	1.50	Mogollón
Timber Peak	10,510				Magdalena Mountains
Sugarloaf	10,505	un 10,580	215	1.25	Brazos
Rosilla Peak	10,500				Las Vegas
Caballo Mountain	10,496				Jémez
Cimarroncito Peak	10,468				Cimarrón
Casita Piedra Peak	10,453				Taos
Cerro Rubio	10,449				Jémez
Sandía Peak	10,447				Sandía Mountains
Shell Mtn. (Sierra de los Valles)	10,445	un 10,347 (Sierra de Toledo)	475	1.25	Valles Calderas
Pajarito Mountain	10,441				Jémez
Capulín Peak	10,416	Palo Encebado Peak	932	1.80	Taos Mountains
Banco Julian	10,413				Tusas
Sierra del Don Fernando	10,363				Fernando Mountains
Black Mountain	10,360				Cimarrón
Brokeoff Mountain	10,357				Tusas
un 10,347 (Sierra De Toledo)	10,347	Cerro Toledo	337	1.75	Valles Calderas
Blue Mountain	10,336				San Mateo Mountains

Peak or Mountain	Elev. (ft.)	Closest Neighbor	Drop	Dist. (mi.)	Range (or Region)
Cerros del Abrigo	10,332				Valles Calderas
un 10,293	10,293	Sacaton Mountain	313	0.45	Mogollón
Vick's Peak	10,252				San Mateo Mountains
Cerro Picacho	10,288				Mora
un 10,281	10,281	South Baldy	325	1.60	Magdalena Mountains
Whitehorse Hill	10,255				Sierra Blanca
Bear Mountain	10,253	un 10,442	273	0.75	Santa Barbara
un 10,245 [6]	10,245	Pajarito Mountain	315	1.25	Jémez
Alegres Mountain	10,244				Mangas
Trail Peak	10,242	un 11,024	497	6.20	Cimarrón (Philmont)
Cerrito Colorado	10,235	Sierra de Don Fernando	310	3.25	Fernando Mountains
Hermit's Peak	10,212				Las Vegas
Apache Peak	10,203				Taos Mountains
Palko Peak (un 10,201) [5]	10,201	Capitán Peak	1,021	5.00	Capitán Mountains
Glorieta Baldy	10,199				Santa Fe
Cerro Grande	10,199				Jémez
Burned Mountain	10,189	Tusas			Tusas
McNight Mountain	10,165				Black Range
Palo Encebado Peak	10,165	Capulín Peak	680	1.80	Taos Mountains
Tusas Mountain	10,143				Tusas
San Mateo Peak	10,139				San Mateo Mountains
Grouse Mountain	10,135				Mogollón
Los Griegos	10,117				Jémez
Mount Withington	10,115				San Mateo Mountains
Indian Peak	10,115	Black Mountain	475	1.00	Mogollón
Cerro Pelado	10,109				Jémez
Thumb	10,107				Sandía Mountains
Manzano Peak	10,098				Manzano Mountains
Ute Peak	10,093				(North Central NM)
Capitán Peak	10,083	Palko Peak (un 10,201)	903	5.00	Capitán Mountains
un 10,057	10,057	Gallo Peak	397	0.85	Manzano Mountains
Cerro de los Posos	10,049	Shell Mountain	339	1.50	Valles Calderas
The Wall	10,039	un 11,611	328	2.00	Cimarrón
Reeds Peak	10,011				Black Range

Peak or Mountain	Elev. (ft.)	Range (or Region)	Peak or Mountain	Elev. (ft.)	Range (or Region)
Hillsboro Peak	10,011	Black Range	Mosca Peak	9,509	Manzano
Gallo Peak	10,003	Manzano Mountains	Horse Peak	9,490	Mangas
Magote Peak	9,987	Tusas	Crosby Mountain	9,483	Dátil
Nogal Peak	9,957	Sierra Blanca	Cerro de la Olla	9,475	(North Central NM)
Burn Peak	9,938	Cimarrón	San Miguel Mountain	9,473	Nacimiento
Rabbit Mountain	9,938	Jémez	Guadalupe Peak	9,450	Manzano
Gomer Mountain	9,938	Mogollón	Bighorn Peak	9,442	Tusas
El Cielo	9,932	Las Vegas	Luera Peak	9,420	Luera
Chromo Mountain	9,925	Chama	O Bar O Mountain	9,410	(Gila National Forest)
Lookout Peak	9,922	Cimarrón	Shaefers Peak	9,400	Cimarrón
Bearwallow Mountain	9,920	Mogollón	Beautiful Mountain	9,388	Chuska
Escondido Mountain	9,869	Quemado	Fox Mountain	9,383	Gallo
Cerro Pedernal	9,862	Jémez	Capilla Peak	9,375	Manzano
North Baldy	9,858	Magdalena	Cerro Pelón	9,367	Jémez
Diamond Peak	9,850	Black Range	Davenport Peak	9,355	Dátil
Grass Mountain	9,841	Santa Fe	Sunset Peak	9,320	Capitán
Rayado Peak	9,805	Cimarrón	Osha Peak	9,313	Manzano
Eagle Peak	9,802	Tularosa	Black Mountain	9,303	(Gila Natl. Forest)
Nacimiento Peak	9,801	Nacimiento	Barillas Peak	9,300	Las Vegas
West Baldy	9,785	Mogollón	Alamo Peak	9,260	Sacramento
South Sandía Peak	9,782	Sandía	Mount Sedgwick	9,256	Zuni
Turkeyfeather Mountain	9,771	Mogollón	Sacramento Peak	9,255	Sacramento
Crater Peak	9,748	Cimarrón	Aspen Peak	9,244	Jémez
Kiowa Peak	9,735	Tusas	Pelona Mountain	9,220	Pelona
Mangas Mountain	9,691	Mangas	Ladrón Peak (West Summit)	9,210	Ladrón
Grassy	9,679	San Mateo	Ruiz Peak	9,208	Jémez
Elk Mountain	9,678	Elk	Ladrón Peak (East Summit)	9,176	Ladrón
Sawyers Peak	9,668	Black (Mimbres)	Atalaya Mountain	9,121	Santa Fe
Monjeau Peak	9,641	Sierra Blanca	Lookout Mountain	9,112	Zuni
Cross-O Mountain	9,620	Black Range	North Peak	9,110	Magdalena
Mining Mountain	9,617	Jémez	Jim Smith Peak	9,100	(Spur Lake Basin)
Bosque Peak	9,610	Manzano	Buck Peak	9,085	Magdalena
Carrizo Mountain	9,605	Jicarilla	East Elk Mountain	9,058	Elk
Madre Mountain	9,556	Dátil	Italian Peak	9,052	Magdalena

Peak or Mountain	Elev. (ft.)	Range (or Region)	Peak or Mountain	Elev. (ft.)	Range (or Region)
Pajarito Peak	9,042	Sierra Nacimiento	Palomas Peak	8,685	Sandía
Cerro del Pino	9,030	Jémez	Piñon Knob	8,677	(Gila National Forest)
Black Peak	9,029	Piños Altos	Gallinas Peak	8,615	(Corona Region)
Organ Needle	9,012	Organ	Cooney Peak	8,600	Mogollón
Grizzley Tooth	9,005	Cimarrón	Zilditloi Mountain	8,573	Chuska
Tooth of Time	9,003	Cimarrón	Clara Peak	8,549	Jémez
Signal Peak	9,001	Piños Altos	Animas Peak	8,532	Animas
Gallina Peak	8,977	(North Central NM)	Patos Mountain	8,508	Sacramento
Salinas Peak	8,958	San Andrés	St. Peters Dome	8,463	Jémez
Lilly Mountain	8,949	Jerky	Baldy Peak	8,445	Organ
Ortiz Peak	8,928	Ortiz	Big Hatchet Peak	8,441	Big Hatchet
Little Squaretop	8,919	Organ	San Francisco Mountain	8,435	San Francisco
Placer Mountain	8,897	Ortiz	Cookes Peak	8,404	Cookes
Lookout Mountain	8,872	Black Range	Cerro Blanco	8,388	Manzano
Organ Peak	8,870	Organ	Sawmill Mesa	8,350	(Northwest NM)
John Kerr Peak	8,868	Tularosa Mtns.	Twin Sisters	8,340	Piños Altos
Apache Mountain	8,868	(Apache National Forest)	Saddle Mountain	8,340	San Francisco
West Mountain	8,842	Capitán	Tucson Mountain	8,308	Sacramento
Whiterocks Mountain	8,827	San Francisco	Squaretop	8,300	Organ
Bay Buck Peak	8,825	San Mateo	Devisadero Peak	8,300	Taos
Laughlin Peak	8,818	(Northeast NM)	Wedge	8,300	Organ
Church Mountain	8,805	Sierra Blanca	San Pedro Mountain	8,242	San Pedro
Chuska Peak	8,795	Chuska	San Andrés Peak	8,241	San Andrés
Dead Man Peak	8,786	(North Central NM)	Oro Quay Peak	8,226	San Pedro
Tecolote Mesa	8,755	(Northwest NM)	Lost Lake Mountain	8,210	Mogollón
South Mountain	8,750	(Albuquerqe Region)	Bearspring Peak	8,195	Jémez
Guadalupe Mountain	8,735	Taos	Tularosa Mountain	8,195	(Apache National Forest)
Oscura Peak	8,732	Oscura	Bear Mountain	8,190	Black Range
Granite Peak	8,731	Diablo	Capulín Mountain	8,182	(Northeast NM)
White Pinnacle	8,730	Diablo	Boundary Peak	8,182	Jémez
Sierra Grande	8,720	(Northeast NM)	Magdalena Peak	8,152	Magdalena
Oso Ridge	8,713	Zuni	Middle Rabbit Ear	8,150	Organ
Bearhead Peak	8,711	Jémez	Sugarloaf	8,150	Organ
Dillon Mountain	8,710	(Apache National Forest)	Rabbit Ear Plateau	8,150	Organ
Seven Brothers Mountain	8,690	Black (Mimbres)	Hellroaring Mesa	8,145	(Apache National Forest)

Peak or Mountain	Elev. (ft.)	Range (or Region)	Peak or Mountain	Elev. (ft.)	Range (or Region)
Lone Mountain	8,145	Jicarilla	Wind Mountain	7,280	Cornudas
East Carrizo Cone	8,128	Sacramento	Cerro Montosa	7,259	Los Piños
Monero Mountain	8,060	(Northwest NM)	Socorro Peak	7,243	Socorro
Boiler Peak	8,048	Black Range	Ship Rock	7,178	(Northwest NM)
Burro Peak	8,035	Burro	Huerfano Peak	7,151	(Northwest NM)
Greer Peak	8,005	San Andrés	Gym Peak	7,106	Florida
North Oscura Peak	7,999	Oscura	Capitol Peak	7,098	San Andrés
Jacks Mountain	7,986	Burro	Cerro Bonanza	7,088	(Cerrillos Region)
Hart Peak	7,978	Cimarrón	Bear Peak	7,087	San Andrés
Thompson Cone	7,932	Black Range	Bullard Peak	7,064	Big Burro
A Four Mountain	7,890	Piños Altos	Center Peak	7,062	Animas
Haystack Mountain	7,871	Black Range	Starvation Peak	7,042	Las Vegas
Seventy-four Mountain	7,818	Mogollón	San Agustín Peak	7,030	San Andrés
Vera Cruz Mountain	7,800	Sacramento	North Baylor Peak	7,018	Organ
Cabezón Peak	7,785	(West Central NM)	Strawberry Peak	7,012	Lemitar
Cedro Peak	7,767	Manzanita	Table Mountain	7,000	Gallinas
Baylor Peak	7,721	Organ	Angel Peak	6,988	(Bloomfield Region)
Mount Washington	7,716	Manzanita	Devoy's Peak	6,740	(Northeast NM)
Jicarilla Peak	7,688	Jicarilla	Alamo Mountain	6,670	Cornudas
Kelly Mountain	7,650	Kelly	Hachita Peak	6,639	Little Hatchets
Guaje Mountain	7,636	Jémez	Magdalena Peak	6,625	Sierra de las Uvas
Monte Largo	7,606	(Albuquerque Region)	Knight Peak	6,602	Big Burro
Saliz Mountains (unnamed)	7,587	Saliz	Sierra de las Uvas	6,601	(Hatch Region)
Monte Negro	7,581	Ladrones	Black Point	6,467	Peloncillo
Timber Mountain	7,565	Caballo	Guadalupe Mountain	6,450	Peloncillo
Sol se Mete	7,541	Manzanita	Bald Mountain	6,396	Little Burro
Whiteface Mountain	7,530	Los Piños	Schoolhouse Mountain	6,370	Big Burro
Reading Mountain	7,490	Piños Altos	Bunk Robinson Peak	6,241	Peloncillo
Cerro Pelón	7,470	Manzanita	Flying W Mountain	6,217	Cedar Mountain
Niggerhead	7,400	Gallinas	Cedar Mountain	6,207	Cedar Mountain
Emery Peak	7,322	(Folsom Region)	Caballo Cone	6,091	Caballo
Gillespie Mountain	7,309	Animas	Wildhorse Peak	6,078	Big Burro
Florida Peak	7,295	Florida	Rabbit Ear Mountain	6,058	(Northeast NM)
Polvadera Mountain	7,292	Lemitar	North Pyramid Peak	6,008	Pyramid
Baxter Mountain	7,285	Sacramento	Fra Cristóbal Mountain	6,003	Fra Cristóbal

Peak or Mountain	Elev. (ft.)	Range (or Region)
Caballo Mountain	5,993	Caballo
Hilo Peak	5,955	Animas
South Pyramid Peak	5,910	Pyramid
Mount Riley	5,905	Potrillo
Doña Ana Peak	5,899	Doña Ana
Robledo Mountain	5,876	Picacho-Robledo
North Sister	5,802	Tres Hermanas
Rimrock Mountain	5,785	Pyramid
Middle Sister	5,786	Tres Hermanas
Cornudas Mountain	5,730	Cornudas
Little Black Peak	5,679	(Carrizozo Region)
South Sister	5,614	Tres Hermanas
Goat Mountain	5,607	Pyramid
Bishop Cap	5,419	(Las Cruces Region)
North Anthonys Nose	5,388	Franklin
Kirk Peak	5,359	Pyramid
Eighty-five Hill	5,105	Pyramid
Aberdeen Peak	5,044	Pyramid
Black Top	5,025	Tres Hermanas
Lee Peak	5,022	Pyramid
Niggerhead	4,993	Pyramid
Picacho Peak	4,959	Picacho-Robledo
Tucumcari Mountain	4,956	(Tucumcari Region)
Swallow Fork Peak	4,954	Pyramid
Tortugas Mountain	4,931	(Las Cruces Region)
Cedar Knob	4,902	Pyramid
Dogs Head	4,812	Pyramid
Guzmans Lookout Mountain	4,762	Potrillo

[1] Though not meeting the criteria, Middle Truchas is ranked.

[2] The actual summit is higher than the named point.

[3] The actual summit a few hundred feet into Colorado.

[4] The named point is 12,739' in elevation, with a 189' foot.
shoulder drop to the actual summit.

[5] Unnamed on many maps.

[6] Height is estimated.

*Cabezón Peak, (7,785') located in the Cabezón Wilderness Study Area,
glows in storm light.*

Peak/Mountain	Elev. (ft.)	Range (or Region)
A Four Mountain	7,890	Piños Altos
Aberdeen Peak	5,044	Pyramid
Agua Fria Peak	11,086	Cimarrón
Alamo Mountain	6,670	Cornudas
Alamo Peak	9,260	Sacramento
Alegres Mountain	10,244	Mangas
Angel Peak	6,988	(Bloomfield region)
Animas Peak	8,532	Animas
Apache Mountain	8,868	(Apache National Forest)
Apache Peak	10,203	Taos Mountains
Ash Mountain (north) [6]	11,240	Cimarrón
Ash Mountain (south)	11,430	Cimarrón
Aspen Peak	11,109	Santa Fe
Aspen Peak	9,244	Jémez
Atalaya Mountain	9,121	Santa Fe
Bald Mountain	6,396	Little Burro
Baldy Mountain	12,441	Cimarrón
Baldy Mountain	12,046	Latir
Baldy Peak	8,445	Organ
Banco Julian	10,413	Tusas
Barillas Peak	9,300	Las Vegas
Baxter Mountain	7,285	Sacramento
Bay Buck Peak	8,825	San Mateo
Baylor Peak	7,721	Organ
Bear Mountain	10,665	Cimarrón (Philmont)
Bear Mountain	10,253	Santa Barbara
Bear Mountain	8,190	Black Range
Bear Peak	7,087	San Andrés
Bearhead Peak	8,711	Jémez
Bearspring Peak	8,195	Jémez
Bearwallow Mountain	9,920	Mogollón
Beautiful Mountain	9,388	Chuska
Big Costilla Peak [4]	12,931	Culebra
Big Hatchet Peak	8,441	Big Hatchet
Bighorn Peak	9,442	Tusas

Peak/Mountain	Elev. (ft.)	Range (or Region)
Big Red (un 11,024)	11,024	Cimarrón
Bishop Cap	5,419	(Las Cruces region)
Black Mountain	11,302	Columbine-Hondo
Black Mountain	10,895	Cimarrón (Philmont)
Black Mountain	10,643	Mogollón
Black Mountain	10,360	Cimarrón
Black Mountain	9,303	(Gila National Forest)
Black Point	6,467	Peloncillo
Black Top	5,025	Tres Hermanas
Blue Mountain	10,336	San Mateo Mountains
Boiler Peak	8,048	Black Range
Bosque Peak	9,610	Manzano
Boundary Peak	8,182	Jémez
Brazos Peak	11,288	Brazos
Brazos Ridge	10,963	Tusas
Brokeoff Mountain	10,357	Tusas
Buck Peak	9,085	Magdalena
Bull of the Woods Mtn.	11,645	Taos
Bullard Peak	7,064	Big Burro
Bunk Robinson Peak	6,241	Peloncillo
Burn Peak	9,938	Cimarrón
Burned Mountain	10,189	Tusas
Burro Peak	8,035	Burro
Caballo Cone	6,091	Caballo
Caballo Mountain	10,496	Jémez
Caballo Mountain	5,993	Caballo
Cabezón Peak	7,785	(West Central NM)
Cabresto Peak	12,448	Latir
Canjilón Mountain	10,913	Tusas
Capilla Peak	9,375	Manzano
Capitán Peak	10,083	Capitán Mountains
Capitol Peak	7,098	San Andrés
Capulín Mountain	8,182	(Northeast NM)
Capulín Peak	12,357	Santa Fe
Capulín Peak	10,416	Taos Mountains

Peak/Mountain	Elev. (ft.)	Range (or Region)
Carrizo Mountain	9,605	Vera Cruz
Casita Piedra Peak	10,453	Taos
Cedar Knob	4,902	Pyramid
Cedar Mountain	6,207	Cedar Mountain
Cedro Peak	7,767	Manzanita
Center Baldy	10,535	Mogollón
Center Peak	7,062	Animas
Cerrito Colorado	10,235	Fernando Mountains
Cerro Blanco	8,388	Manzano
Cerro Bonanza	7,088	(Cerrillos region)
Cerro Chimayosos	12,841	Santa Barbara
Cerro de la Olla	9,475	(North Central NM)
Cerro de los Posos	10,049	Valles Calderas
Cerro del Oso	11,255	Mora
Cerro del Piño	9,030	Jémez
Cerro Grande	10,199	Jémez
Cerro Montosa	7,259	Los Piños
Cerro Olla	11,932	Mora
Cerro Pedernal	9,862	Jémez
Cerro Pelado	10,109	Jémez
Cerro Pelón	9,367	Jémez
Cerro Pelón	7,470	Manzanita
Cerro Picacho	10,288	Mora
Cerro Rubio	10,449	Jémez
Cerro Toledo	10,925	Valles Calderas
Cerro Vista	11,939	Mora
Cerros del Abrigo	10,332	Valles Calderas
Chromo Mountain	9,925	Chama
Church Mountain	8,805	Sierra Blanca
Chuska Peak	8,795	Chuska
Cieneguilla Mountain	10,616	Cimarrón
Cimarróncito Peak	10,468	Cimarrón
Clara Peak	8,549	Jémez
Clear Creek Mountain (Mt. Phillips)	11,730	Cimarrón

Peak/Mountain	Elev. (ft.)	Range (or Region)
Comanche Peak	11,299	Cimarrón
Cookes Peak	8,404	Cookes
Cooney Peak	8,600	Mogollón
Cornudas Mountain	5,730	Cornudas
Crater Peak	9,748	Cimarrón
Crosby Mountain	9,483	Dátil
Cross-O Mountain	9,620	Black Range
Cuchillo de Fernando	11,395	Rincon Mountains
Davenport Peak	9,355	Dátil
Dead Man Peak	8,786	(North Central NM)
Devisadero Peak	8,300	Taos
Devoy's Peak	6,740	(northeast NM)
Diamond Peak	9,850	Black Range
Dillon Mountain	8,710	(Apache National Forest)
Dogs Head	4,812	Pyramid
Doña Ana Peak	5,899	Doña Ana
Eagle Peak	9,802	Tularosa
East Carrizo Cone	8,128	Sacramento
East Elk Mountain	9,058	Elk
East Pecos Baldy	12,529	Truchas
Eighty-five Hill	5,105	Pyramid
El Cielo	9,932	Las Vegas
Elephant Rock	10,556	Latir
Elk Mountain	11,661	Las Vegas
Elk Mountain	9,678	Elk
Emery Peak	7,322	(Folsom Region)
Escondido Mountain	9,869	Quemado
Fairchild (un 12,819)	12,819	Taos
Flag Mountain	11,946	Columbine-Hondo
Florida Peak	7,295	Florida
Flying W Mountain	6,217	Cedar Mountain
Fox Mountain	9,383	Gallo
Fra Cristóbal Mountain	6,003	Fra Cristóbal
Frazer Mountain	12,163	Taos
Gallina Peak	10,893	Columbine-Hondo

Peak/Mountain	Elev. (ft.)	Range (or Region)	Peak/Mountain	Elev. (ft.)	Range (or Region)
Gallina Peak	8,977	(North Central NM)	Jacks Mountain	7,986	Burro
Gallinas Peak	8,615	(Corona region)	Jawbone Mountain	10,960	Tusas
Gallo Peak	10,003	Manzano	Jicarilla Peak	12,494	Truchas
García Peak	10,925	Cimarrón	Jicarilla Peak	7,688	Jicarilla
Gillespie Mountain	7,309	Animas	Jicarita Peak	12,835	Mora
Glorieta Baldy	10,199	Santa Fe	Jim Smith Peak	9,100	(Spur Lake Basin)
Goat Mountain	5,607	Pyramid	John Kerr Peak	8,868	Tularosa Mountains
Gold Hill	12,711	Columbine-Hondo	Kachina Peak (un 12,481)	12,481	Taos
Gomer Mountain	9,938	Mogollón	Kelly Mountain	7,650	Kelly
Granite Peak	8,731	Diablo	Kiowa Peak	9,735	Tusas
Grass Mountain	9,841	Santa Fe	Kirk Peak	5,359	Pyramid
Grassy	10,015	San Mateo	Knight Peak	6,602	Big Burro
Green Mountain	11,165	Cimarrón	La Mosca	11,036	San Mateo
Greenie Peak	11,249	Latir	Ladrón Peak	9,176	Ladrón
Greer Peak	8,005	San Andrés	Lake Fork Peak	12,881	Taos
Grizzley Tooth	9,005	Cimarrón	Lake Peak	12,409	Santa Fe
Grouse Mesa	11,403	Brazos	Larkspur Peak (11,982) [2]	12,014	Taos
Grouse Mountain	10,135	Mogollón	Latir Peak	12,708	Latir
Guadalupe Mountain	8,735	Taos	Laughlin Peak	8,818	(Northeast NM)
Guadalupe Mountain	6,450	Peloncillo	Lee Peak	5,022	Pyramid
Guadalupe Peak	9,450	Manzano	Lew Wallace Peak	12,449	Taos
Guaje Mountain	7,636	Jémez	Lilly Mountain	8,949	Jerky
Guzmans Lookout Mtn.	4,762	Potrillo	Little Black Peak	5,679	(Carrizozo Region)
Gym Peak	7,106	Florida	Little Costilla Peak	12,584	Cimarrón
Hart Peak	7,978	Cimarrón	Little Jicarita Peak	12,266	Santa Barbara
Hatchita Peak	6,639	Little Hatchets	Little South Truchas [6]	12,560	Truchas
Haystack Mountain	7,871	Black Range	Little Squaretop	8,919	Organ
Hellroaring Mesa	8,145	(Apache National Forest)	Lobo Peak	12,115	Columbine-Hondo
Hermit's Peak	10,212	Las Vegas	Lookout Mountain	9,112	Zuni
Hillsboro Peak	10,011	Black Range	Lookout Mountain	8,872	Black Range
Hilo Peak	5,955	Animas	Lookout Peak	11,580	Sierra Blanca
Horse Peak	9,490	Horse	Lookout Peak	9,922	Cimarrón
Huerfano Peak	7,151	(Northwest NM)	Lone Mountain	8,145	Jicarilla
Indian Peak	10,115	Mogollón	Los Griegos	10,117	Jémez
Italian Peak	9,052	Magdalena	Lost Lake Mountain	8,210	Mogollón

Peak/Mountain	Elev. (ft.)	Range (or Region)
Lucero Peak	10,820	Taos
Luera Peak	9,420	Luera
Madre Mountain	9,556	Dátil
Magdalena Peak	8,152	Magdalena
Magdalena Peak	6,625	Sierra de las Uvas
Magote Peak	9,987	Tusas
Mangas Mountain	9,691	Mangas
Manzano Peak	10,098	Manzano Mountains
McNight Mountain	10,165	Black Range
Middle Rabbit Ear	8,150	Organ
Middle Sister	5,786	Tres Hermanas
Middle Truchas [1]	13,060	Truchas
Mining Mountain	9,617	Jémez
Mogollón Baldy	10,770	Mogollón
Monjeau Peak	9,641	Sierra Blanca
Monero Mountain	8,060	(Northwest NM)
Monte Largo	7,606	(Albuquerque region)
Monte Negro	7,581	Ladrone
Mosca Peak	9,509	Manzano
Mount Riley	5,905	Potrillo
Mount Sedgwick	9,256	Zuni
Mount Taylor	11,301	San Mateo
Mount Washington	7,716	Manzanita
Mount Withington	10,115	San Mateo Mountains
Mount Walter	13,133	Taos
Nacimiento Peak	9,801	Sierra Nacimiento
Niggerhead	7,400	Gallinas
Niggerhead	4,993	Pyramid
Nogal Peak	9,957	Sierra Blanca
North Anthonys Nose	5,388	Franklin
North Baldy	9,858	Magdalena
North Baylor Peak	7,018	Organ
North Oscura Peak	7,999	Oscura
North Peak	9,110	Magdalena
North Pyramid Peak	6,008	Pyramid
North Sister	5,802	Tres Hermanas
North Truchas	13,024	Truchas
O Bar O Mountain	9,410	(Gila National Forest)
Old Mike	13,113	Taos
Organ Needle	9,012	Organ
Organ Peak	8,870	Organ
Oro Quay Peak	8,226	San Pedro
Ortiz Peak	11,205	Valle Vidal
Ortiz Peak	8,928	Ortiz
Oscura Peak	8,732	Oscura
Osha Mountain	10,885	Rincón Mountains
Osha Peak	9,313	Manzano
Oso Ridge	8,713	Zuni
Pajarito Mountain	10,441	Jémez
Pajarito Peak	9,042	Sierra Nacimiento
Palko Peak (un 10,201) [5]	10,201	Capitán Mountains
Palo Encebado Peak	10,165	Taos Mountains
Palomas Peak	8,685	Sandía
Patos Mountain	8,508	Sacramento
Pecos Baldy	12,500	Truchas
Pelona Mountain	9,220	Pelona
Peñasco Amarillo	10,712	Tusas
Peñasco Grande	11,931	Las Vegas
Peñascoso Mountain	10,970	Santa Barbara
Penitente Peak	12,249	Santa Fe
Picacho Peak	4,959	Picacho-Robledo
Picurís Mountain	10,810	Picurís Range
Pinabete Peak	11,953	Latir
Piñon Knob	8,677	(Gila National Forest)
Placer Mountain	8,897	Ortiz
Polvadera Mountain	7,292	Lemitar
Polvadera Peak	11,232	Jémez
Pueblo Peak	12,305	Taos

Peak/Mountain	Elev. (ft.)	Range (or Region)
Rabbit Ear Mountain	6,058	(Northeast NM)
Rabbit Ear Plateau	8,150	Organ
Rabbit Mountain	9,938	Jémez
Rayado Peak	9,805	Cimarrón
Reading Mountain	7,490	Piños Altos
Red Dome	12,681	Taos
Redondo Peak	11,254	Jémez
Reeds Peak	10,011	Black Range
Relica Peak	11,784	Columbine-Hondo
Rimrock Mountain	5,785	Pyramid
Robledo Mountain	5,876	Picacho-Robledo
Rosilla Peak	10,500	Las Vegas
Round Mountain	10,809	Pecos
Ruiz Peak	9,208	Jémez
Sacaton Mountain	10,658	Mogollón
Sacramento Peak	9,255	Sacramento
Saddle Mountain	8,340	San Francisco
Salinas Peak	8,958	San Andrés
Saliz Mountains (unnamed)	7,587	Saliz
San Andrés Peak	8,241	San Andrés
San Antonio Peak	10,935	Tusas
San Agustín Peak	7,030	San Andrés
San Francisco Mtn	8,435	San Francisco
San Mateo Peak	10,139	San Mateo Mtns
San Miguel Mountain	9,473	Nacimiento
San Pedro Mountain	8,242	San Pedro
San Pedro Peak	10,605	Sierra Nacimiento
Sandía Crest	10,678	Sandía Mountains
Sandía Peak	10,447	Sandía Mountains
Santa Barbara Pk. (un 12,626)	12,650	Santa Barbara
Santa Fe Baldy	12,622	Santa Fe
Santa Fe Dome	10,613	Santa Fe
Sawmill Mesa	8,350	(Northwest NM)
Sawmill Mountain	10,962	Latir
Sawyers Peak	9,668	Black (Mimbres)
Schoolhouse Mountain	6,370	Big Burro
Seven Brothers Mountain	8,690	Black (Mimbres)
Seventy-four Mountain	7,818	Mogollón
Shaefers Peak	9,400	Cimarrón
Sheepshead	12,696	Truchas
Shell Mountain (Sierra De Los Valles)	10,445	Valles Caldera
Shiprock	7,178	(Northwest NM)
Sierra Blanca Peak	11,973	Sierra Blanca
Sierra de las Uvas	6,601	(Hatch Region)
Sierra del Don Fernando	10,363	Fernando Mountains
Sierra Grande	8,720	(Northeast NM)
Sierra Mosca	11,801	Truchas
Signal Peak	9,001	Piños Altos
Simpson Peak	12,976	Taos
Socorro Peak	7,243	Socorro
Sol se Mete	7,541	Manzanita
South Baldy	10,783	Magdalena Mountains
South Fork Peak	11,978	Taos
South Mountain	8,748	(Albuquerque Region)
South Pyramid Peak	5,910	Pyramid
South Sandía Peak	9,782	Sandía
South Sister	5,614	Tres Hermanas
South Truchas	13,102	Truchas
Spring Mountain	11,180	Las Vegas
Squaretop	8,300	Organ
St. Peters Dome	8,463	Jémez
Starvation Peak	7,042	Las Vegas
State Line Peak [3]	12,867	Culebra
Strawberry Peak	7,012	Lemitar
Sugarloaf	10,505	Brazos
Sugarloaf	8,150	Organ
Sunset Peak	9,320	Capitán

Peak/Mountain	Elev. (ft.)	Range (or Region)	Peak/Mountain	Elev. (ft.)	Range (or Region)
Swallow Fork Peak	4,954	Pyramid	un 10,347 (Sierra De Toledo)	10,347	Valles Calderas
Table Mountain	7,000	Gallinas	un 10,610	10,610	Brazos
Taos Cone	12,277	Taos	un 10,612	10,612	Brazos
Taos Peak	11,220	Taos	un 10,705 [6]	10,705	Tusas
Tecolote Mesa	8,755	(Northwest NM)	un 10,761	10,761	Jémez
Tesuque Peak	12,047	Santa Fe	un 10,970 [6]	10,970	Brazos
Tetilla Peak	10,800	Latir	un 10,980	10,980	Cimarrón
The Dome	11,336	Truchas	un 11,033 [6]	11,033	Valle Vidal
The Knob	10,625	Santa Barbara	un 11,045	11,045	Rincón Mountains
The Wall	10,039	Cimarrón	un 11,055 (Angel Fire Peak)	11,055	Rincón Mountains
Thompson Cone	7,932	Black	un 11,061 [6]	11,061	Brazos
Thompson Peak	10,554	Santa Fe	un 11,067 [6]	11,067	Brazos
Thumb	10,107	Sandía Mountains	un 11,081	11,081	Valle Vidal
Timber Mountain	7,565	Caballo	un 11,100 [6]	11,100	Cimarrón
Timber Peak	10,510	Magdalena Mountains	un 11,116	11,116	Truchas
Tolby Peak	11,527	Cimarrón	un 11,123	11,123	Latir
Tooth of Time	9,003	Cimarrón	un 11,177	11,177	Latir
Tortugas Mountain	4,931	(Las Cruces Region)	un 11,275	11,275	Latir
Touch-Me-Not Mountain	12,045	Cimarrón	un 11,276	11,276	Mora
Trail Peak	10,242	Cimarrón (Philmont)	un 11,312	11,312	Latir
Trampas Peak	12,170	Truchas	un 11,353	11,353	Cimarrón
Trouble	12,622	Mora	un 11,387	11,387	Latir
Tschicoma Mountain (Chicoma)	11,561	Jémez	un 11,385	11,385	Santa Fe
Tucson Mountain	8,308	Sacramento	un 11,375	11,375	Truchas
Tucumcari Mountain	4,956	(Tucumcari Region)	un 11,410	11,410	Santa Fe
Tularosa Mountain	8,195	(Apache National Forest)	un 11,437	11,437	Latir
Tunnel Hill	11,668	Taos	un 11,455	11,455	Las Vegas
Turkeyfeather Mountain	9,771	Mogollón	un 11,500	11,500	Cimarrón
Tusas Mountain	10,143	Tusas	un 11,500 [6]	11,500	Mora
Twin Sisters	8,340	Piños Altos	un 11,571	11,571	Santa Fe
un 10,057	10,057	Manzano Mountains	un 11,611	11,611	Cimarrón
un 10,245 [6]	10,245	Jémez	un 11,656	11,656	Truchas
un 10,281	10,281	Magdalena Mountains	un 11,691	11,691	Mora
un 10,293	10,293	Mogollón	un 11,792	11,792	Columbine-Hondo
			un 11,802	11,802	Columbine-Hondo

|---|---|---|
un 11,821	11,821	Truchas
un 11,849	11,849	Columbine-Hondo
un 11,893	11,893	Columbine-Hondo
un 11,903 [6]	11,903	Truchas
un 11,912	11,912	Taos
un 11,921	11,921	Cimarrón
un 11,979	11,979	Truchas
un 11,981	11,981	Latir
un 11,987	11,987	Truchas
un 12,012	12,012	Taos
un 12,014 (Larkspur Peak) [2]	12,014	Taos
un 12,020 [6]	12,020	Truchas
un 12,025	12,025	Latir
un 12,050 [6]	12,050	Columbine-Hondo
un 12,110 (Doctor Peak)	12,110	Santa Fe
un 12,114	12,114	Truchas
un 12,116	12,116	Latir
un 12,156	12,156	Taos
un 12,165	12,165	Latir
un 12,170 [6]	12,170	Latir
un 12,217	12,217	Columbine-Hondo
un 12,225	12,225	Truchas
un 12,382	12,382	Santa Barbara
un 12,383	12,383	Culebra
un 12,450 [6]	12,450	Culebra
un 12,453	12,453	Truchas
un 12,456	12,456	Latir
un 12,469	12,469	Truchas
un 12,483	12,483	Santa Fe
un 12,496	12,496	Taos
un 12,510	12,510	Mora
un 12,515	12,515	Truchas
un 12,550	12,550	Latir
un 12,728	12,728	Taos
un 12,828	12,828	Mora

Peak/Mountain	Elev. (ft.)	Range (or Region)
un 12,877	12,877	Culebra
un 12,885 [6]	12,885	Truchas
Ute Peak	10,093	(North Central NM)
Vallecito Mountain	12,643	Taos
Van Diest Peak	11,222	Valle Vidal
Venado Peak	12,734	Latir
Vera Cruz Mountain	7,800	Sacramento
Vermejo Peak	11,610	Cimarrón
Vick's Peak	10,252	San Mateo Mountains
Vintrero [4]	12,881	Culebra
Virsylvia Peak	12,594	Latir
Wedge	8,300	Organ
West Baldy	9,785	Mogollón
West Mountain	8,842	Capitán
West Truchas [1]	13,070	Truchas
Wheeler Peak	13,161	Taos
White Pinnacle	8,730	Diablo
Whiteface Mountain	7,530	Los Piños
Whitehorse Hill	10,255	Sierra Blanca
Whiterocks Mountain	8,827	San Francisco
Whitewater Baldy	10,895	Mogollón
Wildhorse Peak	6,078	Big Burro
Willow Mountain	10,783	Mogollón
Wind Mountain	7,280	Cornudas
Zilditloi Mountain	8,573	Chuska

[1] Though not meeting the criteria, Middle Truchas is ranked.

[2] The actual summit is higher than the named point.

[3] The actual summit a few hundred feet into Colorado.

[4] The named point is 12,739' in elevation, with a 189' shoulder drop to the actual summit.

[5] Unnamed on many maps.

[6] Height is estimated.

Toadacheene Lake in the Chuska Mountains, Navajo Nation.

New Mexico is a large state, but it has few large wilderness or roadless areas of more than 100,000 acres. It would behoove us to ask ourselves why. One might say that the eastern third of the state is the plains, but the same is true of Colorado. A better answer would be that there is less of the Big Outside in New Mexico because it has a longer history of habitation by European settlers, is better watered, and offers a better climate for cattle ranching than some of our neighboring states. Many of the lush, better-watered areas of this state have been in use for more than three hundred years. Cattle can be in the high country over a longer season here than in places like Montana or Wyoming. This, of course, necessitates access. Roads have been punched into New Mexico's roadless areas so that things like stock tanks can be built. Much of the landscape has been modified to channel and control our meager water resources.

The following lists were compiled from several sources. Bob Marshall, in the 1930s, was the first to extensively catalog the large remaining roadless tracts in the west. Dave Forman and Howie Wolke updated his list in the 1990s. Bob Julyan's excellent book on New Mexico wilderness filled out the list, including administrative agencies. The list of roadless areas not coverd by either of those sources was compiled by me, using NM BLM Wilderness Coalition and NM Wilderness Alliance resources. The list includes the acreages of declared Wildernesses and WSAs (Wilderness Study Areas) and also of surrounding roadless areas, making it possible to calculate each area's true roadless acreage. Approximate acreages are provided for non-inventoried areas. I identified areas over 10,000 acres in the national forests with a few exceptions.

I make no claim that all the non-inventoried roadless areas are fit for inclusion in the nations' wilderness system. They are merely large remaining tracts of national forest land in New Mexico. If you like the Big Outside, go to these areas and find out for yourself what they are all about.

Our public lands continue to be truncated and not always nobly used, and we are now witnessing the cumulative results of mankind's reckless treatment of the environment. As the wilderness shrinks, so do our opportunities to experience these primal areas. As a landscape photographer, it is increasingly difficult for me to practice my craft in areas that are not protected as wilderness. City lights degrade the night sky and air pollution taints the wonderful vistas that only these areas can provide.

Mike Butterfield

Name & Status	Size (acres)	+Acreage	Total Acres	Location/Administration
ROCKY MOUNTAINS/NORTHEAST				
Pecos Wilderness	222,673	177,000	399,673	Sangre de Cristo Mtns./Santa Fe NF, Carson NF
Latir Peak Wilderness	20,506	146,000	166,506	Sangre de Cristo Mtns./Carson NF
Wheeler Peak Wilderness	19,150	57,000	76,150	Sangre de Cristo Mtns./Carson NF- Questa Ranger District
Chama River Canyon Wilderness	50,300		50,300	Jémez Mtns./Santa Fe NF, Carson NF, BLM Taos Resource District
San Pedro Parks Wilderness	41,132		41,132	Jémez Mtns./Santa Fe NF-Cuba District, Carson NF Coyote Ranger District
Bandelier National Monument	32,727		32,727	Jémez Mtns./National Park Service
Cruces Basin Wilderness	18,902		18,902	Sangre de Cristo Mtns./Carson NF
Dome Wilderness	5,200		5,200	Jémez Mtns./Santa Fe NF
Columbine-Hondo WSA	30,500		30,500	Sangre de Cristo Mtns./Carson NF
San Antonio WSA	7,050	18,050	25,100	Sangre de Cristo Mtns./BLM
Sabinoso WSA	15,760	1,840	17,600	Sangre de Cristo Mtns./BLM
Río Chama WSA	11,985	-6,067	5,918	Sangre de Cristo Mtns./BLM
Valle Vidal Natural Area	100,000	-52,000	48,000	Sangre de Cristo Mtns./Carson NF
Río Grande Wilderness Inv. Unit	9,447	6,653	16,100	Sangre de Cristo Mtns./BLM
Not Inventoried:				
Lobato Mesa Roadless		32,339	32,339	Jémez Mtns./Santa Fe NF
Polvadera Peak Roadless		18,425	18,425	Jémez Mtns./Santa Fe NF
Canjilón (national forest)		18,425	18,425	Tusas Mtns./Carson NF
Bearhead Pk.		18,048	18,048	Jémez Mtns./Santa Fe NF
Jawbone Mtn. Roadless		17,672	17,672	Tusas Mtns/Carson NF
Phillips Mtn.		14,290	14,290	Sangre de Cristo Mtns./NM Parks & Recreation
Mud Spring		14,288	14,288	Jémez Mtns./Santa Fe NF
Canjilón (Private)		12,403	12,403	Tusas Mtns./Private
Policarpio Roadless		11,283	11,283	Rincón Mtns./Carson NF
TOTAL ACREAGE:				
ROCKY MOUNTAINS/NORTHEAST	585,332	505,649	1,090,981	

Name & Status	Size (acres)	+Acreage	Total Acres	Location/Administration
NORTHWEST REGION				
El Malpais National Monument	115,000	263,000	378,000	Western New Mexico/National Park Service
Chaco Culture National Historical Park	36,864		36,864	Western New Mexico/National Park Service
Cebolla Wilderness	62,800		62,800	Western New Mexico/BLM
West Malpais Wilderness	39,700		39,700	Western New Mexico/BLM
Bisti/De-Na-Zin Wilderness (Combined plus Corridor)	37,100		37,100	Western New Mexico/BLM
Ojito Wilderness	11,000		11,000	Western New Mexico/BLM
Boca del Oso WSA Complex	66,401	41,291	107,692	Western New Mexico/BLM
Mesita Blanca and Eagle Peak WSA	66,389	-33,222	33,167	Western New Mexico/BLM
Chain of Craters WSA	15,200	2,240	17,440	Western New Mexico/BLM
Petaca Pinta WSA	11,668	3,012	14,680	Western New Mexico/BLM
Cabezón WSA	8,159		8,159	Western New Mexico/BLM
Ah-Shi-Sle-Pah WSA	6,563		6,563	Western New Mexico/BLM
Techado Mesa Wilderness Inventory Unit	19,000	17,580	36,580	Western New Mexico/BLM
Oso Ridge Roadless (Not Inventoried)		13,158	13,158	Zuni Mtns./Cíbola NF
Mt Taylor Roadless		10,150	10,150	Mt Taylor/Cíbola NF
TOTAL ACREAGE: NORTHWEST REGION	495,844	317,209	813,053	
CENTRAL REGION				
Sandía Mountain Wilderness	37,232		37,232	Central Río Grande/Cíbola NF
				Tijeras Ranger District
Manzano Mountain Wilderness	36,970		36,970	Central Río Grande/Cíbola NF
				Mountainair Ranger District
Little San Pascual, Chupadera,				
and Indian Wells Wilderness (Combined)	30,287		30,287	Central Río Grande/US Fish and Wildlife Service
Robledo Mtns. and				
Las Uvas Mtns. WSA (Combined)	23,563	186,437	210,000	South Central Desert Region/BLM
Sierra Ladrones WSA	45,308	54,936	100,244	Central Río Grande/BLM
Organ Mtns. WSA	7,283	57,709	64,992	South Central Desert Region/BLM
Presilla, Las Canas, Veranito, and Stallion WSA	40,962		40,962	Central Río Grande/BLM
Jornada del Muerto WSA	31,147	5,700	36,847	Central Río Grande/BLM
Antelope WSA	20,710	-2,601	18,109	Central Río Grande/BLM
Caballo Mtns. Wilderness Inv. Unit	28,800		28,800	South Central Desert Region/BLM
Big Yucca Wilderness Inv. Unit	5,460	-260	5,200	Central Río Grande/BLM

Name & Status	Size (acres)	+Acreage	Total Acres	Location/Administration
San Andrés Mtns. South Roadless Area	240,000		240,000	White Sands Missile Range
San Andrés Mtns. Central Roadless Area		155,000	155,000	Central Río Grande/White Sands Missile Range
San Andrés Mtns. North Roadless Area		155,000	155,000	Central Río Grande/White Sands Missile Range
Sawyers Peak Roadless Area		121,000	121,000	Dátil-Mogollón Plateau/White Sands Missile Range
Los Piños Mtns. Roadless (Not Inventoried)		23,686	23,686	Central Río Grande/Sevilleta NWR
TOTAL ACREAGE: CENTRAL REGION	393,282	1,037,898	1,431,180	
SOUTHEAST REGION				
White Sands National Monument	147,500		147,500	East Central Region/National Park Service
White Mountain Wilderness	48,873	92,000	140,873	East Central Region/Lincoln NF Smokey Bear Ranger District
Capitán Mountain Wilderness	35,822		35,822	East Central Region/Lincoln NF Smokey Bear Ranger District
Carlsbad Caverns National Park Wilderness	33,125		33,125	Desert Southeast/National Park Service
Salt Creek Wilderness	9,621		9,621	Desert Southeast/US Fish and Wildlife Service
Sacramento Escarpment (Proposed Wilderness)	50,840		50,840	Desert Southeast/BLM, Lincoln NF
Pup Canyon (Proposed Wilderness)	43,900		43,900	Desert Southeast/BLM, Lincoln NF
Last Chance Canyon (Proposed Wilderness)	27,380		27,380	Desert Southeast/BLM, Lincoln NF
Rawhide Canyon (Proposed Wilderness)	26,400		26,400	Desert Southeast/BLM, Lincoln NF
West Potrillo Mtns., East Potrillo Mtns., Mount Riley, and Aden Lava Flow WSA (Combined)	159,972	128,585	288,557	South Central Desert Region/BLM
Guadalupe Escarpment WSA	20,936	117,000	137,936	Desert Southeast/Lincoln NF
Brokeoff Mtns. WSA	31,606	34,744	66,350	Desert Southeast/BLM
Little Black Peak and Carrizozo Lava Flow WSA (Combined)	25,312	20,771	46,083	East Central Region/BLM
Culp Canyon WSA	10,937	3,525	14,462	Desert Southeast/BLM
Devils Den Canyon, McKittrick Canyon, and Lonesome Ridge WSA (Combined)	4,025		4,025	Desert Southeast/BLM
Mudgetts WSA	2,941	549	3,490	Desert Southeast/BLM
Sacramento Rim Roadless (Alamo Peak) Not Inventoried		18,425	18,425	Sacramento Mtns./Lincoln NF
TOTAL ACREAGE: SOUTHEAST REGION	679,190	415,599	1,094,789	

Name & Status	Size (acres)	+Acreage	Total Acres	Location/Administration
SOUTHWEST REGION				
Gila Wilderness	558,060	166,500	724,560	Dátil-Mogollón Plateau/Gila NF-Wilderness
				Glenwood Ranger Districts
Aldo Leopold Wilderness	202,016	198,000	400,016	Dátil-Mogollón Plateau/Gila NF
				Black Range Wilderness Ranger Districts
Apache Kid Wilderness	44,650	86,000	130,650	Dátil-Mogollón Plateau/Cibola NF
				Magdalena Ranger District
Blue Range Wilderness	29,304		29,304	Dátil-Mogollón Plateau/Gila NF
Withington Wilderness	18,869		18,869	Dátil-Mogollón Plateau/Cíbola NF
				Magdalena Ranger District
Continental Divide WSA	68,761	101,239	170,00	Dátil-Mogollón Plateau/BLM
Cowboy Springs WSA	6,999	33,990	40,989	Desert Southwest/BLM
Cookes Range WSA	19,608	4,240	23,848	Desert Southwest/BLM
Blue Creek WSA	14,896	6,760	21,656	Dátil-Mogollón Plateau/BLM
Gila Lower Box WSA	8,555	11,040	19,595	Dátil-Mogollón Plateau/BLM
Hell Hole WSA (Tillie Hall Peak)	18,680		18,680	Dátil-Mogollón Plateau/Gila NF
Whitmire Canyon WSA	18,000		18,000	Desert Southwest/Coronado NF
Devils Backbone WSA	8,904	6,280	15,184	Dátil-Mogollón Plateau/BLM
Lower San Francisco WSA	8,800		8,800	Dátil-Mogollón Plateau/Gila NF
Horse Mountain WSA	5,032	3,240	8,272	Dátil-Mogollón Plateau/BLM
Apache Box WSA	932	5,297	6,229	Dátil-Mogollón Plateau/BLM
Gila Middle Box Wilderness Inv. Unit	19,660	21,985	41,645	Dátil-Mogollón Plateau/BLM, Gila NF
Devils Creek Roadless Area	100,000		100,000	Dátil-Mogollón Plateau/Gila NF
Not Inventoried:				
Eagle Peak Roadless		92,870	92,870	Tularosa Mtns./Gila NF
Madre Mtn. Roadless		72,947	72,947	Dátil Mtns./Cíbola NF
Magdalena Mtns. Roadless		58,656	58,656	Magdalena Mtns./Cíbola NF
San Franciso Mtns. Roadless		50,384	50,384	San Francisco Mtns./Apache NF
Big Burro Mtns. NF Roadless		45,497	45,497	Dátil-Mogollón Plateau/Gila NF
Gallinas Mtns. Roadless		43,993	43,993	Dátil Mtns./Cíbola NF
Bear Mtns. Roadless		43,993	43,993	Dátil Mtns./Cíbola NF
Escondido Mtn. Roadless		37,977	37,977	Apache NF/Apache NF

Name & Status	Size (acres)	+Acreage	Total Acres	Location/Administration
Not Inventoried:				
John Kerr Pk.		31,584	31,584	Tularosa Mtns./Gila NF
Black Range Roadless (Bear Mtn.)		32,710	32,710	Black Range/Gila NF
Long Canyon		31,208	31,208	Tularosa Mtns./Gila NF
Apache Mtn. Roadless		26,323	26,323	Apache NF/Apache NF
O-Bar-O Mtn. (national forest)		24,441	24,441	Dátil-Mogollón Plateau/Gila NF
Fox Mtn. Roadless		22,560	22,560	Gallo Mtns./Apache NF
Crosby Mtns. Roadless		22,560	22,560	Dátil Mtns./Cíbola NF
Big Burro Mtns. State Roadless		22,182	22,182	Dátil-Mogollón Plateau/State of NM, BLM
Saddle Mtn. Roadless		20,670	20,670	San Francisco Mtns./Apache NF
Elk Mtn.		17,672	17,672	Elk Mtns./Gila NF
Sawtooth Mtns. Roadless		13,913	13,913	Dátil Mtns/Cíbola NF
Tillie Hall Peak Roadless - Arizona Portion		12,787	12,787	Dátil Mogollón Plateau/Apache NF
Mangas Mtn. Roadless		12,032	12,032	Dátil Mogollón Plateau/Apache NF
Largo Creek		12,032	12,032	San Francisco Mtns./Apache NF
O-Bar-O Mtn. (state land)		9,024	9,024	Dátil-Mogollón Plateau/State of NM, BLM
TOTAL ACREAGE: SOUTHWEST REGION	1,051,731	1,502,736	2,554,317	
BOOTHEEL REGION				
Peloncillo Mtns. Wilderness Complex (Proposed Wilderness)	194,513		194,513	Desert Southwest/BLM, Forest Service
Lordsburg Playa (Proposed Wilderness)	35,860		35,860	Desert Southwest/BLM
Cedar Mtns. WSA	14,911	158,010	172,921	Desert Southwest/BLM
Big Hatchet Mtns. WSA	48,720	100,000	148,720	Desert Southwest/BLM
Alamo Hueco Mtns. WSA	16,264	15,720	31,984	Desert Southwest/BLM
Florida Mtns. WSA	22,336		22,336	Florida Mtns./BLM
Bunk Robinson WSA	7,000		7,000	Desert Southwest/Coronado NF
Animas Mtns. Roadless Area		60,010	60,010	Desert Southwest/Nature Conservancy, BLM
TOTAL ACREAGE: BOOTHEEL REGION	339,604	333,740	673,344	
TOTAL ALL REGIONS	3,459,423	4,071,390	7,530,813	